SANT KABIR'S
**Way to
Emotional Intelligence**

SANT KABIR'S
Way to
Emotional Intelligence

Rashmi Soni

STERLING PAPERBACKS
An imprint of
Sterling Publishers (P) Ltd.
Regd. Office: A1/256 Safdarjung Enclave,
New Delhi-110029. CIN: U22110DL1964PTC211907
Tel: 26387070, 26386209; Fax: 91-11-26383788
E-mail: mail@sterlingpublishers.com
www.sterlingpublishers.com

Sant Kabir's
Way to Emotional Intelligence
© 2017, Dr. Rashmi Soni
ISBN 978 93 86245 07 6

All rights are reserved.
No part of this publication may be reproduced, stored in a retrieval system or transmitted, in any form or by any means, mechanical, photocopying, recording or otherwise, without prior written permission of the author.

Printed in India

Printed and Published by Sterling Publishers Pvt. Ltd.,
Plot No. 13, Ecotech-III, Greater Noida - 201306,
Uttar Pradesh, India

Foreword

It is with great pleasure that I write a few paragraphs about this book of Dr. Rashmi Soni. She has titled it *Sant Kabir's Way to Emotional Intelligence*. On an instant response to this title, one may wonder what Sant Kabir had to do with Emotional Intelligence. Most of us are used to looking upon Kabir as a poet who was very controversial in his time and yet was loved by all communities. His couplets (*Dohe*) are still as popular or may even be more popular today than they may have been in his own time. A good number of us understand their meaning, too, but generally do not care about their depth of meaning and relevance to our day-to-day life.

I, myself, grew like that till I was influenced by Kabir's personality in my first visit to Maghar, where Kabir is said to have died. He wanted to challenge the popular belief that death at Maghar was a sure way to hell, as opposed to death in Varanasi which ensured heaven. He deliberately migrated to Maghar during his last days. One is not sure whether Kabir went to hell or heaven after his death, but the fact is that he is revered by all and is proving even more relevant today as we advance in the modern times of science and technology.

When I read Kabir with this frame of mind, he became my mentor. Each couplet of his gave me a deep meaning and an answer to all conflicts of life. This resulted in equanimity (*Samatva*) in my life and no challenge of life could disturb me. Though it took some time in fruition, once imbibed there was no dilemma any more. I wanted to share this conviction with others and this led to the creation of *Kabir Peace Mission* in 1990. The word "peace" here meant an integrated development leading to peace all around. The Mission highlighted the fact that human life is a rare privilege and it should be lived with a missionary zeal.

Dr. Rashmi Soni is a modern-day educationist, as well as a psychologist. She has a long experience in teaching and has come across thousands of young students. As a compassionate person, she tried to understand them closely, rather than judge them as most of us do. She observed that despite all the success in academics and career, a good number of the students were not happy and suffered from multiple problems. The modern-day psychologists only address their problems at a surface level and may be giving temporary relief to them. However, Dr. Rashmi goes deeper into the source of the problem and proposes solutions which address the root cause rather than just the effects. This book is the result of her deep contemplation.

(2)

Fundamentally, human psyche has remained the same since ancient times. Each one of us wants to be loved, understood, appreciated, and encouraged. But in the race today, most of us have no time even for ourselves, what to say for others. The result is that today, a human being is a lonely creature amidst a crowd of so-called well-wishers. We get a large number of greetings, messages, gifts, etc., on occasions like birthdays, festivals, anniversaries, and others, but none of them gives us eternal peace. After a temporary joy, we revert to the state of loneliness. Dr. Soni has been successfully able to relate Kabir to this inner need of human beings and shares it through this book.

Rashmi came in my contact only about two years ago, but has become closer to me and my family than many decades-old contacts. She also became a life member of

Foreword

Kabir Peace Mission and has endeared herself to everyone in this setup within a short period. She has faced problems in life like all of us do, but her response to them has been an example for all to emulate. This resulted in acquisition of finer human qualities, which is what we call high Emotional Intelligence. In this acquisition, Rashmi found Kabir to be very relevant and has successfully related Kabir and Emotional Intelligence. Hence, the book is titled as *Sant Kabir's Way to Emotional Intelligence*. I congratulate Rashmi for her maiden effort in this field.

The publisher of this book, Sterling Publishers of New Delhi, is closely known to me for more than 25 years. All my English books have been published by Sterling and, in a way, Mr. S. K. Ghai made me an author. He always encourages new writers if they write for the betterment of the society. He has very rightly encouraged Rashmi by publishing this book. I feel that it is just a beginning for her as an author and much more will come from her pen in future.

With these words, I once again congratulate Rashmi and wish her the best.

Lucknow
Date: 17 April, 2017
Mobile: 9415015859

Rakesh K. Mittal
Chief Coordinator
Kabir Peace Mission

Foreword

Emotion is the main guiding force of every living creature. That's why EQ (Emotional Quotient) of every being is governed by the heart and head respectively. Swami Vivekananda said that whenever we have a conflict between the Head and the Heart, we should follow the Heart.

In the Bhagavat Gita, the Lord says that the almighty is seated in the core of the heart of all beings and is guiding them through His power (Maya) just as a mechanic operates a machine.

Those who are predominately intellectual follow the path of knowledge (Jnana) in their spiritual life, whereas those who are rather emotional usually prefer the way of Bhakti (Devotion/Love). However, it is said that emotion without intelligence is blind, whereas intelligence without emotion is lame, meaning both are complementary to each other. The ideal is to combine both knowledge and devotion, in a balanced manner, which was illustrated in the life of Sri Ramakrishna: he was "two in one".

While chronologically presenting "the sages of India", Swami Vivekananda said, "The time was ripe for one to be born who in one body would have the brilliant intellect of Shankara and the wonderfully expansive, infinite heart of Chaitanya . . . who would harmonize all conflicting sets, not only in India but outside of India, and bring a marvellous harmony, the universal religion of head and heart into existence. . . . He was a strange man, this Ramakrishna Paramhansa . . the fulfilment of the Indian sages".[1]

Sant Kabir, too, ideally harmonized both Jnana and Bhakti, giving equal importance to both, as has been very aptly expressed in his oft quoted couplet (Doha):

Nirgun Mera Baap, Sagun Ma Tahari
Kako Nindo Kako Bando, Dono palla Bhari

---
1. *Complete Works of Swami Vivekananda*, Vol. 3, p. 267.

(The God without qualities is my Father, while the God with qualities is my Mother. Whom to praise, whom to blame, both weigh the same.)

Dr. Rashmi Soni, a born educationist, has realized the importance of harmonizing both these aspects towards the complete development of our personality and made a sincere effort in her maiden publication entitled *Sant Kabir's Way to Emotional Intelligence*, to make people realize the reality of life and how to inculcate it "by simply understanding and following the concepts expressed in the Dohas of Kabir Das".

In order to develop a model of ideal personality, Dr. Rashmi Soni has made an in-depth study of this subject and successfully implemented the fruits of her research through her series of personality development workshops designed for young men and women.

It has already been observed that students undergoing these workshops are being immensely benefitted in transforming their lives in a much more meaningful way than it was ever before.

This is why it gives me immense pleasure to write the Foreword of this book. On the one hand, the book presents the intricate philosophy in a very lucid manner and on the other it helps the common people, especially the students and the youth, to elevate their lives through the teachings of the illustrious personality, Sant Kabir Das.

I am confident, this volume will go a long way in positively motivating one and all, whoever go through these encouraging pages, and definitely inspire the author to come out with similar holistic publications in the near future.

May the blessings of the Almighty be showered on Dr. Rashmi Soni and her book galore!

Ramkrishna Mission Sevashram
Vivekananda Polyclinic and
Institute of Medical Sciences
Vivekananda Puram, Lucknow-226007
E-mail: rkmvplko@gmail.com,
rkml@ramakrishnalucknow.org
22 April, 2017

Swami Muktinathananda
Secretary

Acknowledgements

It is a pleasure to express my thanks and gratefulness to all those people whose encouragement, support, and advice shaped this book in important ways.

At the outset, my sincere and deep sense of gratitude goes to my spiritual Guru, Poojniya Swami Muktinathananda, Secretary Ram Krishna Mission, Lucknow, whose benign blessings, love, and motivation has given me courage to face the challenges of life. I am also grateful to Shri. R. K. Mittal ji, who, as a father figure, has always stood by my side and has always guided me. In fact, the idea of correlating the concepts of Emotional Intelligence and dohas of Kabir Das struck my mind the very day when I joined the Kabir Peace Mission two years ago, with the blessings of Mittal Sir. I also need to be grateful to Dr. Anshumali Sharma Ji, who has also been a constant source of inspiration to me for writing this book.

I would like to specially mention the name of Dr. Usha Kumari, my colleague and senior Professor in B.Ed. Department of Mahila College, whose guidance and deep knowledge helped me in understanding the dohas. I cannot forget my dear students who have constantly inspired me to write something for them. Their love and regard for me encouraged me to put my thoughts into words. I am thankful to Mr. Neeraj Pandey also, who helped me in typing the dohas in Hindi.

I am also grateful to Mr. Sanjiv Sarin for taking pains in editing the book. My acknowledgements would be incomplete without paying my thanks and gratitude to

Shri. S. K. Ghai Ji and the whole team of Sterling Publishers for taking interest in the subject matter and publishing this book. It is because of him that my views and thoughts have reached my readers.

Last, but not the least, I should emphasize that my parents have been a constant source of support and understanding throughout the long period of my work. They have always stood beside me in every walk of life and have motivated and inspired me whenever I felt unsure. As ever, my work is always dedicated and devoted to my parents, all my well-wishers, my friends, my teachers, the guiding light of my life, and my loving students.

I sincerely extend my warm wishes to the present and the next generation of children and youth and invite them to share my thoughts in the book. Please come forward to connect with me.

Om Shanti!

Dr. Rashmi Soni
+919415063105
(rashmi_psychologist2003@yahoo.co.in)

Preface

Kabir was a people's poet, educated only by the company of wise men (*Satsang*), and was a keen observer and thinker. He is well known for putting sophisticated concepts in a simple language. Many of his couplets (dohas) and stanzas (*chand*) pertain to observations and advice to make life richer and relevant for the individual and the society. Taken together, these pearls of wisdom are components of what is known as Emotional Intelligence. In this book, we explore the relationship between the sublime poetry of Kabir Das as applied to Emotional Intelligence.

This book is an outcome of a two-fold inspiration. The first inspiration came to me, as an author, from my students to write something on Emotional Intelligence and Personality Development. The second inspiration was from the confidence I gained after having imparted many motivational and counselling sessions, that this book might inspire all people, irrespective of their age.

Being a motivational speaker, I have had the opportunity to conduct a number of sessions on different aspects of Personality Development to a varied audience, from different walks of life. Additionally, being a psychological counsellor, helping and facilitating adults, children, and adolescents in resolving their personal and emotional problems, enabled me to gain a deeper insight into human behaviour and the issues arising due to emotional ill-health or lack of emotional wisdom. Most of the people that I came across were facing relationship oriented problems, either in their personal or professional lives. But my insight told me that their main issue was their problem in understanding the relationship with their *own real self.* Hence, from my experience with people, during the course of all interactions, I arrived at the basic cause of the problem—our lack of clear understanding and sensitivity to ourselves and others.

There exists immense knowledge, potential, capability, and ability within all of us, but we do lack the power of understanding. We rarely use our wisdom. And this is where the concept of Emotional Intelligence becomes pertinent. There is an urgent need today for us to be emotionally intelligent so that we can not only handle our problems and stresses in life positively and intelligently, but can also adjust and work for the welfare of our society with a positive attitude towards life.

The world today needs emotionally intelligent leaders, parents, teachers, children, and youth. Human beings are becoming more cognitively intelligent and advancing in science and technology, but at the same time, they are increasingly facing emotional issues in their professional and personal lives. They are gaining more knowledge but not wisdom. They are connecting more to Internet and less to Inner Net.

The concept of emotional intelligence is an important area of psychological research, especially with regard to how it affects the productivity and success of people. In fact, many experts believe that a person's emotional quotient (EQ) may be more important than their intelligence quotient (IQ) and is certainly a better predictor of success, quality of relationships, and overall happiness. We, as humans, are undoubtedly emotional beings, but we lack the wisdom to understand our emotions and that of others, too, and often do not know when, where and how to express them.

We hear of incidents of people reacting out of proportion in anger, leading to some very hideous and unbelievable results. When in love with someone, people tend to become possessive and want control over that person. There are also growing cases of intolerant students and youth killing people in the spur of a moment, out of intense rage. This clearly shows the hyperactive emotions in today's society. Hence, there is a need to understand, express, and control emotions in a sensitive and wise manner.

Every human being is suffering from three deadly emotions, that is, guilt, fear, and doubt. We have fear and doubt about our future; we fear about being rejected by our own people; we doubt our own potential. Thus, each one of us is suffering from false ego, insecurity, depression, confusion, anxiety, fear, and other mental conflicts and problems. We keep brooding about our past mistakes and incidents.

The ultimate goal of every human being is to have peace and harmony in life, and to be happy and satisfied. However, unfortunately, there is a clear lack of it. Why? Probably, we have contradictions in our convictions. We say we are not angry, but our blood might be boiling in anger; we say we are understanding, but we still face conflicts in relationships; we say we are patient, but many times we might get thoughts of hurting others or ourselves for some reason or the other. We need to be satisfied. We perhaps know when, where, how, what, and why about peace and happiness, but we are still unable to achieve them due to lack of power to control our emotions, to keep our desires and expectations under control.

I feel that every person, irrespective of their knowledge about the subject of psychology and human behaviour, should understand what being emotionally intelligent means. We should know what the concept of Emotional Intelligence is, how a person can become emotionally intelligent, and how he or she can improve upon their day-to-day living and relationships. There are various ways to gain this knowledge, and in my view the age old dohas of Sant Kabir Das are an excellent method.

In India we are usually connected to the roots of our culture, values, and traditions. In addition to many sages and gurus of India, Sant Kabir's influence on our lives has been immense. For most of us, his dohas have been part of our school curriculum, either by way of reading or listening in musical form. I would like to quote a doha that has been so common that each one of us is familiar with it from our childhood:

> ऐसी बानी बोलिये, मन का आपा खोय।
> औरन को शीतल करै, आपौ शीतल होय।।

We learnt the meaning or the so called '*bhavarth*' of this doha in our school days, perhaps then for the purpose of the examination only. But now we realize that many dohas of Kabir Das are about Emotional Intelligence, the way for living a healthy, positive life, with healthy relationships. Through his dohas we can understand the ultimate reality of human life, that is, to connect to the Divine, the Almighty. His dohas, since hundred of years, have been speaking about the core aspects of our personality, like satisfaction in life, importance of communication, time management, positive attitude, fear, love, anger, optimism, pessimism, forgiveness, and so on.

This book, *Sant Kabir's Way to Emotional Intelligence*, is an effort to communicate about the reality of life—the concept and importance of Emotional Intelligence and how we can develop it in us by simply understanding and following the concepts expressed in the dohas of Kabir Das.

A life organized in such a manner that it helps in the discovery of the potential already existing within us and which disciplines our behaviour so as to nurture and nourish them, is a life that is worth living. Our success depends upon the amount of transformation we can successfully bring about in our personality and character. Our present and future success and happiness depends upon ourselves. We are the architects of our own future.

Preface

What we regularly encourage and consistently cultivate in our mind determines, to a great extent, our character, personality and, ultimately, our destiny. An intelligent choice of thoughts can transform the character pattern in us and so the entire destiny is in our own hands. It depends on how successfully we manage and understand our own and others' emotions and feelings.

I accept the limitation that only a few dohas of Kabir Das could be included in this book. However, with the help of around ninety dohas, my aim has been to share the concept of Emotional Intelligence in a very simple way so that the readers can practically apply these simple principles of life in their daily living and bring peace, satisfaction, and happiness in their life and relationships. I request that all the readers try to apply these principles and see for themselves. You will definitely see a change.

I hope this book serves as an inspiration for the youth of today so that they can empower themselves to transform themselves to develop a more positive personality. I wish all my readers, children, and youth, great success in life, a positive and a happy life. It will be a great pleasure if my dear readers come forward to share their views on the topic and give their feedback so that I can improve upon the concept and reach out to more and more people.

Om Shanti!

Dr. Rashmi Soni

Contents

Foreword by
   Shri. R. K.Mittal (Retd. IAS),
     Founder of Kabir Peace Mission   v

Foreword by
   Swami Muktinathananda, Secretary,
   Ram Krishna Mission, Lucknow   ix

Acknowledgements   xi

Preface   xiii

First Realization
   Sant Kabir and Emotional Intelligence   1

Second Realization
   Losing Connection with Nature and Self:
   The Reality of Life   9

Third Realization
   Understanding Emotional Intelligence   21

Fourth Realization
   Love and Acceptance   35

Fifth Realization
   Connection with the Self and the Divine:
   Power of Satisfaction   55

Sixth Realization
  Connecting Sweetly: The Power of Effective
  Communication and Humility   69

Seventh Realization
  Healthy Relationships   83

Eighth Realization
  Don't Worry, Be Happy!   91

Ninth Realization
  Emotional Intelligence and Well Being:
  The Power of Positive Attitude   101

References   129

First Realization

Sant Kabir and Emotional Intelligence

Sant Kabir and Emotional Intelligence

Sant Kabir is well known as a saint to the world and a great poet to millions. A city located at the banks of river Ganga named Varanasi gave world one of the most inspirational poets ever. He is a universal guru and his views about egalitarianism and equality still gives goose bumps to people and have influenced them to an extreme level.

The simplicity of his views has always amazed the world. All of his teachings are in the form of two-liners also called as dohas or couplets. They were written in simple Hindi of that time and the clarity of his thoughts explained in these couplets shakes up our souls. Kabir will always be remembered as a great poet. Unfortunately today, in this hi-tech era, his dohas are losing most of their charm as people are busy in the mad race of life. These couplets do not only have the old magic but are also applicable in everyday life as basic human values and principles. He may have written these couplets years ago, but his writings still give lessons for life.

Kabir was not an educated person but still he has given the world an ocean of knowledge and realizations that can change the life of a person. He created dohas to teach the lesson of humanity to human beings. If the simple principles of life engrained in his dohas are internalized and followed by all of us we can become more positive, feel happier and motivated to make our lives better.

Sant Kabir has influenced our lives since ages. His dohas have given us a philosophy of life which if followed can make our lives peaceful and successful. The world needs today emotionally intelligent leaders, parents, teachers, children, and youth. It is a great predicament that human beings are becoming cognitively intelligent day by day, technologically advanced to the extremes, but what about their being emotionally intelligent? They are becoming knowledgeable but not *understanding*. They are connecting more to Internet and less to Inner Net. So the need of the hour is to develop Emotional Intelligence, that is, the power and wisdom to use their emotions intelligently in different situations of life.

We are all engaged in a mad rat race in today's world. This is a world of competition and technology, and unfortunately no more a world of values, emotions and sensitivity. Humans have become inhuman,

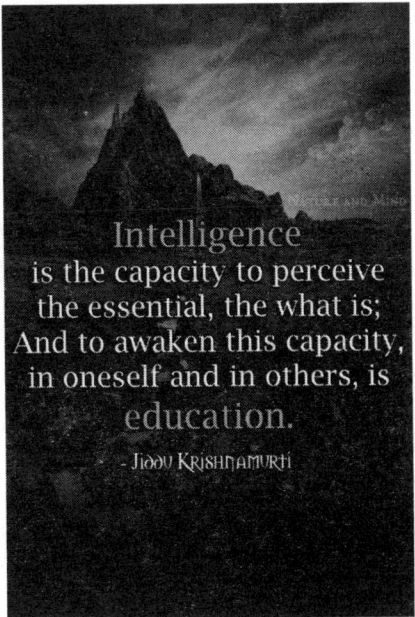

Intelligence is the capacity to perceive the essential, the what is; And to awaken this capacity, in oneself and in others, is education.

- Jiddu Krishnamurti

immoral, valueless, and insensitive towards everything around them. It is said that *Sangati ka asar hota hai* and so we are increasingly being influenced by machines all around us and thus have become a machine ourselves — physically and emotionally. Education and technology are making humans more mechanical than emotional.

The great philosopher and educationist J. Krishnamurti said that education is not only learning from books, memorizing some facts, but also learning how to enjoy the beauty of the environment, how to listen to what the books are saying, whether they are saying something true or false. Education is not just to pass examinations, take a degree and a job, get married and settle down, but also to be able to listen to the birds, to see the sky, to see the extraordinary beauty of a tree, and the shape of the hills, and to feel with them, to be really, directly in touch with them. As we grow older, the sense of listening and seeing, unfortunately, disappears because we have worries, we want more money, a better car and a better mobile — "the smarter one", more children or less children — "that too smarter ones". We become jealous, ambitious, greedy, and envious; so we lose the sense of the beauty of nature. Education should make us more aware — aware about ourselves and our environment.

> There is no need to education. It is not that you read a book, pass an examination, and finish with education. The whole of life, from the moment you are born to the moment you die, is a process of learning.
>
> — Jiddu Krishnamurti, Indian Philosopher

Once somebody asked Krishnamurti that the world is full of callous people, indifferent people, and cruel people and so how can we change those people? Krishnamuri simply replied, which applies very appropriately to the content of this book, "*Why do you bother about changing others? Change yourself. Otherwise as you grow up you will also become callous, indifferent, and cruel.*"[2] Yes, it is so true. We want to change everybody except ourselves. However, the need is to connect more with ourselves and to change ourselves and start walking on the path of self transformation right away.

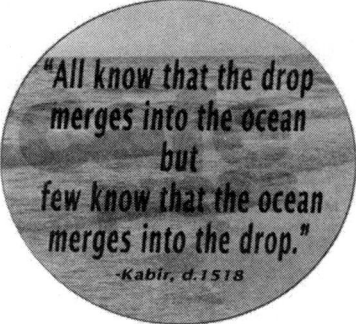

---

2. Krishnamurti, J., *On Education*, Krishnamurti Foundation of India, Chennai (1974), p. 7-8.

Kabir is a very important figure in India. He is unusual as he is spiritually significant to Hindus, Sikhs, and Muslims alike. Kabir openly criticized all sects and gave a new direction to Indian philosophy. Kabir touches the soul, the conscience, and the sense of awareness and the vitality of existence in a manner that is unequalled in both simplicity and style. It is for this reason that Kabir is held in high esteem by everyone.

Another beauty of Kabir's poetry is that he picks up situations that surround our daily lives. Thus, even today, Kabir's poetry is relevant and helpful in both social and spiritual context.[3] Following Kabir means understanding our inner self, realizing ourself, accepting ourself as we are, and becoming harmonious with our surroundings and with people around, leading to becoming emotionally intelligent beings.

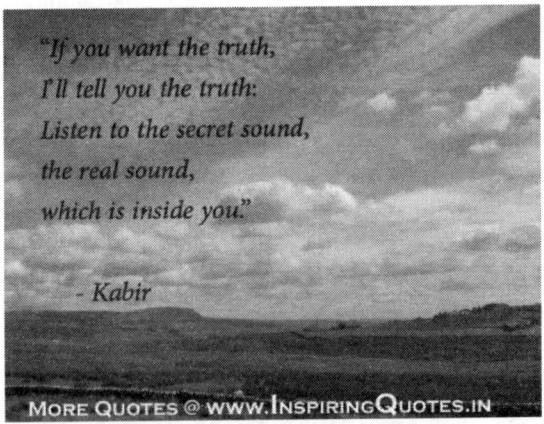

In *Srimad Bhagwad Gita*, the holiest scripture of all scriptures written for humankind, the essence of life has been sermonized by Lord Krishna himself, for living a meaningful, religious, superior, devout, and complete life, a life that takes the ordinary humans towards a transcendental life to release them from earthly existence and merge into heavenly bliss, to become one with the Ultimate God.

---

3. http://chandrakantha.com/articles/indian_music/kabir.html (accessed on 06 March 2017).

"Anyone who is steady in his determination for the advanced stage of spiritual realization and can equally tolerate the onslaughts of distress and happiness is certainly a person eligible for liberation."

– A.C. Bhaktivedanta Swami Prabhup da,
The Bhagavad Gita

"The happiness which comes from long practice, which leads to the end of suffering, which at first is like poison, but at last like nectar - this kind of happiness arises from the serenity of one's own mind."

– Krishna-Dwaipayana Vyasa, The Bhagavad Gita

Kabir was also a lover of God. Having attained the highest form of spiritual experience, which is God-realization. He was fully competent to guide others on the path. Spirituality was a way of life for him. Kabir's main concern was that whatever he did, it was to seek the grace of the Divine power. His dohas guide us through this path of self-realization and ultimately to the realization of the Lord.

Kabir's dohas proclaim simple principles of life which, if internalized and made part of life and daily living, can give us ultimate *happiness, peace* and *tranquillity*. Once we become happy, have peace of mind, and attain satisfaction with life, we can become intelligent emotionally as well. To understand and develop emotional intelligence, we need to realize the reality of ourselves and our present world. So let us together understand the Reality of Life.

... Though this body has its beginning and end, the dweller in the body is infinite and without end. Knowing this, stand up and fight! Not one step back, that is the idea. ... Fight it out, whatever comes. Let the stars move from the sphere! Let the whole world stand against us! Death means only a change of garment. What of it? Thus fight! You gain nothing by becoming cowards. ... Taking a step backward, you do not avoid any misfortune.

... Arise! Awake! Stand up and fight!

(excerpt from Swami Vivekananda's lecture on the Gita : - THE GITA II, Complete Works of Swami Vivekananda)

REALIZATIONS

1. *We human beings are gradually becoming more mechanical than emotional.*
2. *We are connecting more to the Internet than Inner Net.*
3. *Human beings are becoming more knowledgeable than understanding, i.e., cognitively more intelligent than emotionally intelligent.*
4. *The goal of education is not just to pass examinations and earn degrees. Rather, it is to become aware of ourselves and the environment; to connect to ourselves and the divine.*
5. *Sant Kabir Das, a great saint and inspirational poet to millions, gave simple principles of life through his dohas which, if understood and followed in our daily lives, can help us live an emotionally intelligent life.*

Second Realization

Losing Connection with Nature and Self: The Reality of Life

Losing Connection with Nature and Self: The Reality of Life

Let us just think about ourselves and then of people around us for a few minutes. Most of us are simply running every day and every moment of our lives—and for what? A very philosophical question! For satisfaction and happiness, isn't it? *Zindagi aur rishton ko is tarah for granted le chuke hain hum ki zindgi ki daur main hum shayad doosron se kya, apno se hi judna bhool gayen hain.* We are failing, day after day, to connect with ourselves, to our significant others, to people around us, in the large world and, of course, with nature *prakriti* given to us by the Divine God or rather which is God itself. This world is full of vibrations—whatever we eat, drink, breathe, all is made of the vibrations around us. And if we stop for a moment and analyze, we can see for ourselves that everything is becoming negative. So whatever we eat, drink, breathe—everything is made of these negative vibrations.

Deviation from nature is deviation from happiness.
—Samuel Johnson

In today's age of high technology, research shows that our hunger for the natural world still endures. In fact, our connections with nature could just be the best medicine for people of all ages—improving our health, happiness, and well-being. Those same connections could also heal the planet. Research suggests that contact with nature can be beneficial, for example, leading to improvements in mood, cognition, and health.[4]

Research reveals that environments can increase or reduce our level of stress, which in turn impacts our bodies. What we see, hear, and experience at any moment influences not only our mood, but how our nervous, endocrine, and immune systems are working. The stress of an unpleasant environment can cause us to feel anxious or sad or helpless. This in turn elevates our BP, heart rate, and muscle tension and suppresses our immune system. A pleasing environment reverses that absolutely; and regardless of age or culture, humans find nature pleasing. In one study cited in the book *Healing Gardens*, researchers found that more than two-thirds of people choose a natural setting to retreat to when stressed. The above fact correctly applies to the influence of media today on the innocent minds of small children. What they see on small and big screens, they try to follow in their behaviour with others. Children watching all types of cartoon characters, somewhere or the other, unconsciously start living these characters.

Being in nature, or even viewing scenes of nature, reduces anger, fear, and stress and increases pleasant feelings. Exposure to nature not only makes us feel better emotionally, it contributes to our physical well being, reducing blood pressure, heart rate, muscle tension, and the production of stress hormones. It may even reduce mortality, according to scientists such as public health

---

4. https://www.psychologytoday.com/blog/the-moment-youth/201403/does-nature-make-us-happy (accessed on 06 March 2017).

researchers Stamatakis and Mitchell (2008).[5] Research done in hospitals, offices, and schools has found that even a simple plant in a room can have a significant impact on stress and anxiety.

In addition, nature helps us cope with pain. Because we are genetically programmed to find trees, plants, water, and other nature elements fascinating, we are absorbed by nature scenes and forget our pain and discomfort. This is nicely demonstrated in a classic study of patients who underwent gallbladder surgery; half had a view of trees and half had a view of a wall. According to the physician who conducted the study, Robert Ulrich, the patients with the view of trees tolerated pain better, appeared to nurses to have fewer negative effects, and spent less time in the hospital.[6]

One of the most intriguing areas of current research is the impact of nature on general well being. In one study in *Mind*, 95% of those interviewed said their mood improved after spending time outside, changing from depressed, stressed, and anxious to more calm and balanced. Other studies by Ulrich, Kim, and Cervinka (2012) show that time in nature or scenes of nature are associated with a positive mood, and psychological well being, meaningfulness, and vitality.[7]

Furthermore, time in nature or viewing nature scenes increases our ability to pay attention. Because humans find nature inherently interesting, we can naturally focus on what we are experiencing out in nature. This also provides a respite for our over active minds, refreshing us for new tasks.

---

5. Mitchell, R., and F. Popham, (2008), "Effect of exposure to natural environment on health inequalities: An observational population study", *Lancet*, 372 (9650), p. 1655–1660.
6. Ulrich, R. S., (1984), "View through a window may influence recovery from surgery", *Science*, 224 (4647), p. 420–421.
7. Ulrich, R. S., R. F. Simons, B. D. Losito, E. Fiorito, M. A. Miles, and M. Zelson, (1991), "Stress recovery during exposure to natural and urban environments", *Journal of Environmental Psychology*, 11(3), p. 201–230.

"Nature deprivation," a lack of time in the natural world, largely due to hours spent in front of TV or computer screens, has been associated, unsurprisingly, with depression. More unexpected are studies by Weinstein and others that associate screen time with loss of empathy and lack of altruism. And the risks are even higher than depression and isolation.[8] In a 2011 study published in *Journal of the American College of Cardiology*, time in front of a screen was associated with a higher risk of death, and that was independent of physical activity! It was found in a survey that people watch TV approximately 17 hours in a week, i.e., 2 ½ hours every day. This means that every day people lose or waste 20% of their active time on watching television.

Few people would disagree that our natural and cognitive worlds have grown disconnected. Most of us, particularly children, spend far less time in nature today

---

8. Weinstein, N. (2009), "Can nature make us more caring? Effects of immersion in nature on intrinsic aspirations and generosity", *Personality and Social Psychology Bulletin*, 35, p. 1315.

than in the past. There are no required classes in *nature connectedness* in our schools, nor is nature a well-utilized tool for teaching kids to critically think about the world around them. New research, however, suggests that our relationship with nature may be deeply linked to our happiness.⁹

We don't have to look far into history to know that humans evolved in natural settings and were deeply connected to their ecological environments. In the eighteenth century, poet and writer, Samuel Johnson, wisely stated, "Deviation from nature is deviation from happiness." Could those natural settings not only become an avenue by which we find happiness in the twenty-first century, but also provide new psychological insights that help motivate generations toward environmental sustainability?

---

9. https://www.takingcharge.csh.umn.edu/enhance-your-wellbeing/environment/nature-and-us/how-does-nature-impact-our-wellbeing (accessed on 06 March 2017).

Think of the food that we eat each day. There is no single day when we don't hear and read that every food item is now contaminated with poisonous particles, with chemicals. Nothing is pure these days—so what should we eat? The predicament is that despite the fact that we know the truth, we all are eating and drinking impure food—Why? Because we have to!

Humanity is becoming negative day after day. The incidences of violence, corruption, rapes, molestation, and murder prove the fact that sensitivity in people is dying each moment. Last year, over three lakh women were kidnapped, raped, molested—and in some extreme cases, killed—by men across the country. That's almost a 27% increase since 2012—and a year since the world's attention was drawn to the problem of sexual violence against women in India. In 2013, almost 34,000 women were raped. That's a 35.2% rise from 2012, with the highest rate of increase in Delhi.[10]

---

10. http://www.huffingtonpost.in/2014/12/16/crime-against-women-india_n_6330736.html (accessed on 06 March 2017).

Emotions are being murdered every day; selfishness, greed, egoism and narcissism (self love) is what is important these days. We are least bothered about what other persons feel and think. Their emotions are unimportant to us.

India, the richest country in the world in culture, civilization, and values from time immemorial, has larger number of youth. It is a matter of great concern for all of us that this major part of our population is gradually becoming senseless, emotionless, and valueless day by day. The generations that are coming up are totally technological and are least imbued with human principles. And I think that this is the main reason why our youth are becoming more and more depressed, anxious, violent, aggressive, intolerant, suicidal, and murderers. They are the most confused group of people with a lot of conflicts and contradictions in their decisions and feelings. They are directionless youth with no focus and no balance of emotions. The youth are being influenced by media to a great extent. This is reflected in the lifestyle of young people today—the way they act, dress, interact, and the way they want to live their lives.

The question that arises is that despite being educated or for that matter despite being knowledgeable, where is the intelligence of the people, where is their common sense? I think that although our youth today are very intelligent, very learned, and qualified, it is sad that they are not emotionally intelligent, or rather I should say that they don't have an understanding power. *Hum budhiman to bahut ho gaye hain par shayad samajhdar nahi hain!* We have become emotionless, insensitive, lack sympathy (*sahanubhuti*) and empathy (*anubhuti*), and have become more apathetic (*udaseen*) and are not concerned about anything unless it matters to ourselves.

"It is not the strongest of the species that survives, nor the most intelligent, but the one most responsive to change."

— *Charles Darwin*

Dear readers, you must be thinking that I am very negative. Right from the start, I am portraying a negative picture. But I would like to share that I am a very positive person. I believe in positive thoughts and vibrations. I would like to quote here William James, the famous psychologist, when he said that *"the greatest discovery of my generation is that people can alter their lives by altering their thoughts."* I have just tried to put forward the reality that the world is facing today and we cannot escape from this reality. It is all around us.

"Human beings can alter their lives by altering their attitudes of mind."

William James

    Understanding this grave picture of the present society and understanding the importance that emotions play in a person's life, whether in relationships or in professional field, we just need to take up simple human relations principles, simple philosophy of life and apply it in our daily lives and see the consequences. These principles do work! For this, what better than Kabir's dohas, which provide us with simple and practical philosophy of life. Each doha of Sant Kabir, if understood and followed in our daily life, can help us to resolve our conflicts and live a peaceful and happy life. Even if we take one doha each day and keep it in our pocket or purse and live it for that day, we will see an immense change in us and in the people around us.

    Sant Kabir has a unique and a special place in Hindi *sahitya*. He explained big and complex things in a very simple and comprehensible language and manner. By understanding the dohas of Kabir Das, we can very easily understand what we should do and what we should not do. He emphasized basically that all religion are one. People fight in the name of religion, but they fail to understand that God is one and equal for all.

Before we understand the simple principles of Emotional Intelligence in the dohas of Kabir, it becomes important to understand and become aware about the concept of Emotional Intelligence. So let us together explore these two terms.

Every individual has divine powers. The divine power latent in you is limitless.

~ Baba ~

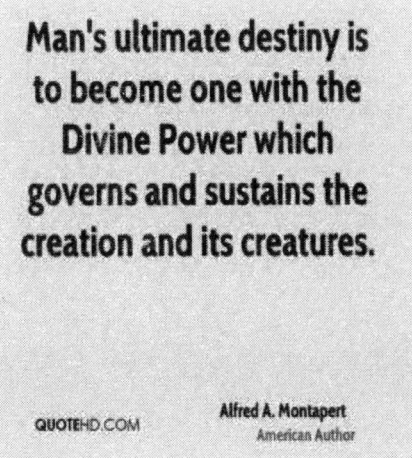

Man's ultimate destiny is to become one with the Divine Power which governs and sustains the creation and its creatures.

Alfred A. Montapert
American Author

REALIZATIONS

1. *We are all running in a rat race in this world, running only after materialistic things to find the ultimate happiness and satisfaction which unfortunately we don't get at the end of the day.*
2. *Connection with nature is the best medicine for all ages to improve health, happiness, and well being.*
3. *People are mostly suffering from psychosomatic diseases—diseases which have psychological reasons.*
4. *The environment and humanity is becoming negative day by day; it is full of negative vibrations. Emotions are being murdered and people are becoming insensitive, leading to broken relationships and mental diseases and problems.*
5. *There is an urgent need to become emotionally intelligent and understanding so that we can understand our own emotions and that of others and live a healthy life with a positive attitude.*

Third Realization

Understanding Emotional Intelligence

Understanding Emotional Intelligence

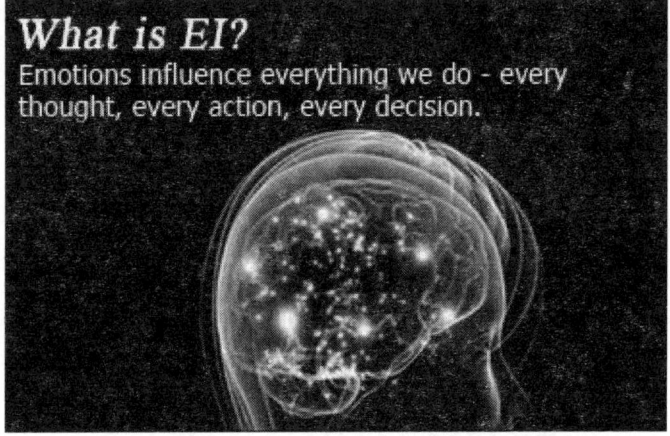

"I don't want to be at the mercy of my emotions. I want to use them, to enjoy them, and to dominate them."

– Oscar Wilde

Emotions are such that sometimes you should abstain from them, and sometimes you should express them. You can't take extreme views here. You cannot always suppress your emotions and you cannot always keep expressing your emotions. Both will bring you difficulties and trouble. If you always suppress your emotions, you will be in trouble. If you always keep expressing your emotions, then also you will be in trouble and you will put others also in trouble. That's why emotions should be streamlined through wisdom. When there is wisdom then you know which emotion to express and which not to express—and where you should express, and where you should not. So you have to use your judgement—where, when, or how you must express your emotions and where it is not wise to do so.

It is undoubtedly our daily experience that there are number of instances and situations when emotions put us in trouble. For example, someone says something to us that is hurting. We immediately react, fall into unending arguments, verbal or even physical abuses, and ultimately all this creates a very messy situation, leading to a lot of stress, conflicts, and broken relationships. We have always learnt to react rather than respond. It has become so natural for us to act and react without becoming aware, without getting conscious, and without applying our wisdom. What is the result? Guilt, humiliation, fear, insecurity, and everything negative that we can think of! And all this, for what?

Emotions seem to rule our daily lives. We make decisions based on whether we are happy, angry, sad, bored, or frustrated. We choose activities and hobbies based on the emotions they incite. "An emotion is a complex psychological state that involves three distinct components: a *subjective experience*, a *physiological response*, and a *behavioural* or *expressive response*." (Hockenbury & Hockenbury, 2007).[11]

➤ The Subjective Experience

While experts believe that there are a number of basic universal emotions that are experienced by people all over the world regardless of background or culture, researchers also believe that experiencing emotion can be highly subjective. While we might have broad labels for certain

---

11. http://mo-issa.com/2016/11/5-factors-that-rule-our-emotional-well-being/ (accessed on 06 March 2017).

emotions such as "angry," "sad," or "happy," our own unique experience of these emotions is probably much more multidimensional. Consider anger. Is all anger the same? Our own experience might range from mild annoyance to blinding rage.

In addition, we don't always experience "pure" forms of each emotion. Mixed emotions over different events or situations in our lives are common. When faced with starting a new job, we might feel both excited and nervous. Getting married or having a child might be marked by a wide variety of emotions, ranging from joy to anxiety. These emotions might occur simultaneously, or we might feel them one after another.

➤ The Physiological Response

When our stomach churns from anxiety or our heart palpitates with fear, then we realize that emotions also cause strong physiological reactions. Many of the physical reactions we experience during an emotion such as sweating palms, racing heartbeat, or rapid breathing are controlled by the sympathetic nervous system, a branch of the autonomic nervous system. The autonomic nervous system controls involuntary body responses such as blood flow and digestion. The sympathetic nervous system is charged with controlling the body's fight-or-flight reactions. When facing a threat, these responses automatically prepare our body to flee from danger or face the threat head-on.

➤ The Behavioural Response

The final component is the actual expression of emotion. A significant amount of time of our daily life is involved in interpreting the emotional expressions of the people around us. Our ability to accurately understand these expressions is tied to what psychologists call Emotional Intelligence and these expressions play a major part in our overall body language. Researchers believe that many expressions are universal, such as a smile indicating happiness or pleasure and a frown indicating sadness or displeasure.[12]

The exploration of Emotional Intelligence and its impact on the interpersonal relationships and human psyche in modern times has so far been credited to Goleman's EQ model where he propagates the self and its supreme acceptance by the individual mind by making self-awareness, self-assertiveness and self-love as the centre piece of all interpersonal relationships, be it in the social sphere, the work area, or the dealing and living with people skills.[13]

The term Emotional Intelligence is an oxymoron. It is sometimes strange to accept the two terms together— *emotional* and *intelligent* at the same time? How is it possible? It is a common thinking that we can either be emotional or intelligent but not Emotionally Intelligent.

---

12. https://www.verywell.com/what-are-emotions-2795178 (accessed on 06 March 2017).
13. http://www.academia.edu/6264444/THE_BHAGAVAD_GITA-Emotional_Intelligence_in_the_Teachings_of_Lord_Krishna_ (accessed on 06 March 2017).

Emotional Intelligence

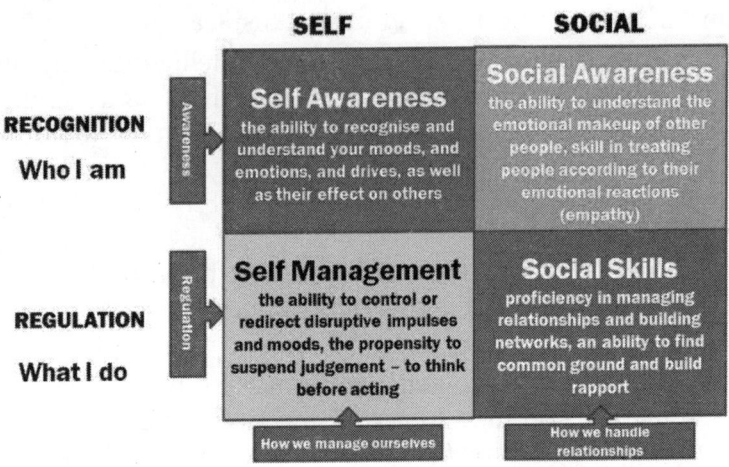

There is little doubt that cognitive intelligence or IQ (Intelligence Quotient) is important in helping us to be successful in life, but it is not the only thing which helps us achieve in life. Emotional Intelligence is considered by a number of writers as more important than intellectual intelligence. Goleman (1996) said "IQ offers little to explain the different destinies of people with roughly equal promises, schooling, and opportunity."

Educational institutions only sharpen the intellectual faculties of individuals which control their intellectual abilities and deal with objective things. But far more precious things are centred on the right side of the brain, which deals with emotions (heart) and governs relationship with people (subjective in nature). A group of individuals can be trained with equal capabilities in objective things by training them in technical matters, new processes, and such other things, but training a group of individual's with equal managerial capabilities (which deal with managing emotions of ourselves and dealing with those of others) may not be possible or may be very difficult.

It is a proven fact that technical qualifications and all degrees and knowledge play only a secondary role when it comes to being successful in career and effective in relationship. *What is that one thing that plays such an important role?* Of course, it is our *attitude*, our emotions, our life skills, our Emotional Intelligence. Almost 80% of our success depends on Emotional Intelligence. A leader however intellectual he or she may be, cannot effectively manage their organization without cultivating the needed Emotional Intelligence.

Many of us find it increasingly difficult to connect in the modern world, both with ourselves and others. An important factor in our ability to successfully connect is Emotional Intelligence. When it comes to happiness and success in our relationships, careers, and personal goals, it is for sure that Emotional Intelligence (EQ) matters just as much as the more well known, intellectual ability (IQ). We need Emotional Intelligence to turn intention into action, in order to make informed decisions about the things that matter most to us, and to connect to others in productive and nurturing ways.[14]

What to do?

1. Learn to recognize and pay attention to all your emotions.
2. Incorporate emotions in your decision-making process.
3. Stay in the present without planning the future or analysing the past.
4. Be aware of the nonverbal messages you send others.
5. Use humour and playfulness to relieve stress.

---

14. https://www.helpguide.org/articles/emotional-health/emotional-intelligence-eq.htm (accessed on 06 March 2017).

In very simple terms, being emotionally intelligent means to be understanding, to be sensitive towards our own emotions and the emotions of others. In more simple terms, it means to become *samajhdaar* (wise) at the intellect level.

Emotions are feelings acted outwardly. For example, when we are feeling hurt, frustrated, or irritated, we express these feelings by becoming angry, that is, we react and either hurt ourselves or others with our actions and reactions. Now the person who stops, pauses, thinks, and understands the reasons, causes, and the intensity of his feelings, why he or she is feeling so, how far he or she is the source for such feelings, will be able to express their feelings in a balanced manner — in other words, in a healthy way. We can also say that such a kind of person knows how to respond rather than react. They will not get into unreasonable arguments or react in a negative manner. They will take care not to hurt themselves or the feelings of the other person. Such a person will be, in a true sense, an emotionally healthy and an emotionally intelligent person.

Emotional intelligence is an essential part of the whole person.

Emotionally intelligent people have a certain way of thinking, feeling, and behaving. They are naturally confident. They bring out the best in others. With an emotionally intelligent person, we feel like he or she is completely interested in us; they are not distracted when talking with us; we get full attention from them. Such a person does not panic but remains focussed on solutions. We can identify emotionally intelligent people pretty quickly. They are the people who:

1. Successfully manage difficult situations
2. Express themselves clearly
3. Gain respect from others
4. Influence other people
5. Attract other people to help them out
6. Keep cool under pressure
7. Recognize their emotional reactions to people or situations
8. Manage themselves effectively
9. Motivate themselves
10. Know how to be positive even during difficult situations.

The ability to take care of our bodies and especially to manage our stress, which has an incredible impact on our overall wellness, is very closely related to our Emotional Intelligence. Only by being aware of our emotional state and our reactions to stress in our lives can we hope to manage stress and maintain good health. Emotional intelligence affects our attitude and outlook on life. It can also help to alleviate anxiety and avoid depression and mood swings. A high level of Emotional Intelligence directly correlates to a positive attitude and happier outlook on life. Emotional intelligence is, in lay person's terms, our level of ability to:[15]

> Recognize and understand our emotions and reactions (self-awareness)
> Manage, control, and adapt our emotions, mood, reactions, and responses (self-management)
> Harness our emotions to motivate ourselves to take appropriate action, commit, follow-through, and work towards the achievement of our goals (motivation)
> Recognize the feelings of others, understand their emotions, and utilize that understanding to relate to others more effectively (empathy)
> Build relationships, relate to others in social situations, lead, negotiate conflict, and work as part of a team (social skills)

By better understanding and managing our emotions, we are better able to communicate our feelings in a more constructive way. We are also better able to understand and relate to those with whom we are in relationships. Understanding the needs, feelings, and responses of those we care about leads to stronger and more fulfilling relationships. When we can identify people's emotions and empathize with their perspective, it's much easier to resolve conflicts or possibly avoid them before they start. We are also better at negotiation due to the very nature of our ability to understand the needs and desires of others.

Higher Emotional Intelligence helps us to become strongly internally motivated, which can reduce procrastination, increase self-confidence, and improve our ability to focus on a goal. It also allows us to create better networks of support, overcome setbacks, and persevere with a more resilient (strong) outlook. Our ability to delay gratification and see the long-term consequences directly affects our ability to succeed. The ability to understand

---

15. http://www.lifehack.org/articles/lifestyle/the-10-essential-habits-of-positive-people.html (accessed on 06 March 2017).

what motivates others, relate in a positive manner, and to build stronger bonds with others in the workplace inevitably makes those with higher Emotional Intelligence better leaders. An effective leader can recognize what the needs of his people are, so that those needs can be met in a way that encourages higher performance and workplace satisfaction. An emotionally understanding and intelligent leader is also able to build stronger teams by strategically utilizing the emotional diversity of their team members to benefit the team as a whole.[16]

Emotional intelligence plays a very critical role in the overall quality of our personal and professional lives, more critical even than our actual measure of brain intelligence. While tools and technology can help us to learn and master information, nothing can replace our ability to learn, manage, and master our emotions and the emotions of those around us.[17]

> "Emotional intelligence is a way of recognising, understanding, and choosing how we think, feel, and act. It shapes our interactions with others and our understanding of ourselves. It defines how and what we learn; it allows us to set priorities; it determines the majority of our daily actions. Research suggests it is responsible for as much as 80% of the "success" in our lives."
>
> - Jensen, Rideout, Freedman & Freedman.

Simply put, Emotional Intelligence is that "something" within us that help us to sense how we feel and enables us to truly connect with others and form a bond. It gives us the ability to be present and listen to someone when they most need it. Emotional Intelligence is that sense of internal

---
16. http://www.lifehack.org/articles/communication/emotional-intelligence-why-important.html ((accessed on 06 March 2017).
17. https://www.skillsyouneed.com/general/emotional-intelligence.html (accessed on 06 March 2017).

balance within us that enables us to keep our composure, make good and right decisions, communicate successfully and effectively, and maintain effective leadership even when under stress. The four main skills of Emotional Intelligence are:

➢ self-awareness – our ability to perceive our emotions and understand our tendencies to act in certain ways in given situations
➢ social awareness – our ability to understand the emotions of other people (what others are thinking and feeling)
➢ self-management – our ability to use awareness of our emotions to stay flexible and direct our behaviour positively and constructively
➢ Relationship management – our ability to use our awareness of our own emotions and those of others to manage interactions successfully.

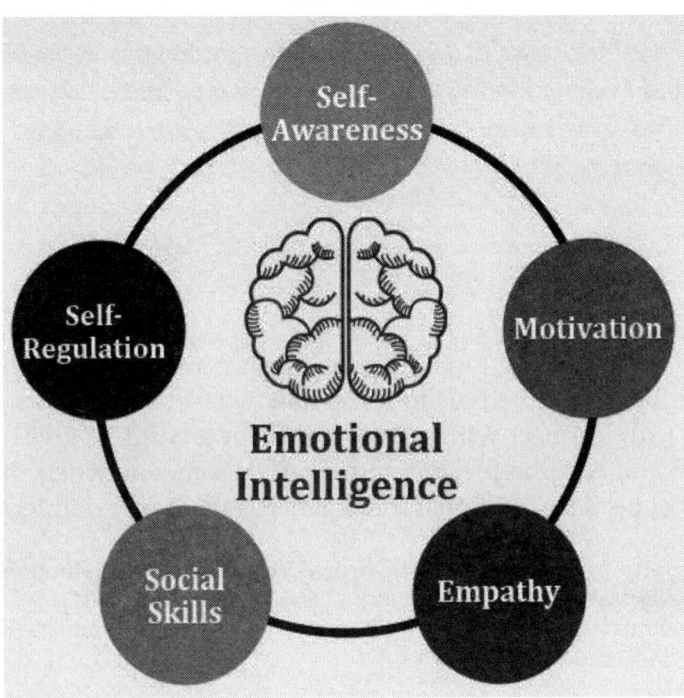

Understanding Emotional Intelligence

To be sure, it's our soft skills that put people at ease, helps them feel appreciated, and enable us to build and maintain solid relationships founded on confidence and trust. And yes, being friendly and likable matters a lot, too! And when we increase our effective use of Emotional Intelligence, we increase our ability to develop more solid, trusting relationships. Thus, we need to understand the importance of Emotional Intelligence, and make it a high priority to develop it in ourselves.

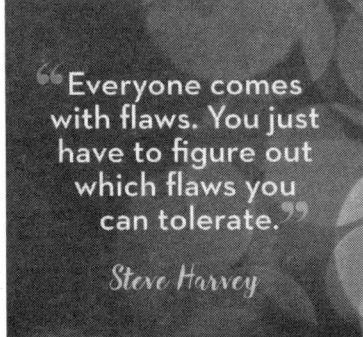

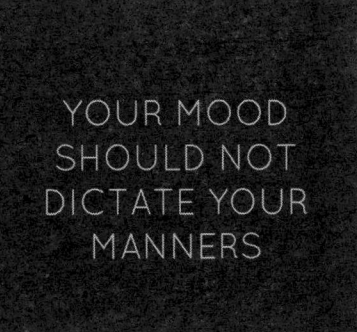

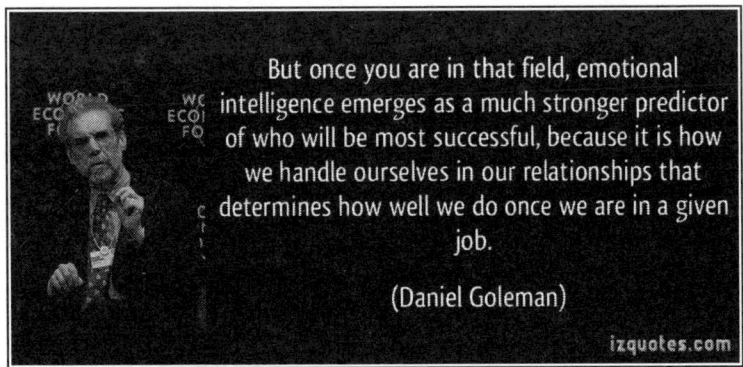

REALIZATIONS

1. *Emotions influence everything we do—every thought, every action, and every decision. But emotions need to be streamlined through wisdom.*
2. *Any emotion involves three distinct components subjective experiences, a physiological response, and behavioural and expressive response.*
3. *Experiencing emotion can be highly subjective. We cannot bind emotions in few labels like angry, sad, or happy; rather, emotions are multidimensional and range from high to low.*
4. *Emotions also cause physical reactions which prepare our body to fight or flight.*
5. *Emotions are also expressed in action. Emotions are expressions of feelings. How accurately we understand the expression of these emotions and ultimately the feelings underlying these emotions in ourselves and in others is Emotional Intelligence.*

Fourth Realization

Love and Acceptance

> I love you.
>
> And it's not because you make me happy,
> not because you make me feel special,
> nor because you're the sweetest person ever,
>
> but because I just love you.
> And I don't need any reasons for that.

Love and Acceptance

Now that we have understood the concept and meaning of Emotional Intelligence and how it is so important in all aspects of our lives, including our success and happiness in life, we need to understand simple principles which, if internalized and followed in our daily life, can help us in becoming Emotionally Intelligent. They can make our life smooth and happy and our relationships positive. What better than dohas of Kabir Das to understand Emotional Intelligence through simple principles of life!

The essence of Emotional Intelligence can be understood from the following doha of Kabir:

पोथी पढ़ि पढ़ि जग मुआ, पंडित भया न कोय।
ढाई आखर प्रेम का, पढ़े सो पंडित होय।।

This doha says that nobody can become intelligent by reading big and heavy books. We can become learned and knowledgeable, but not intellectual, sensible, or understanding. Kabir Das says that a person who understands love and who feels love and compassion for everyone else, is intelligent and knowledgeable in the real sense. Understanding our own emotions and the emotions of others is Emotional Intelligence. Love actually means accepting the other person as he or she is; and before accepting the other person, we need to accept ourselves—including all our strengths and weaknesses.

Love is our basic nature—a natural quality that the Divine Power has instilled in us. When God created us, He instilled love as an integral part of our nature. A newborn baby is full of love. In fact, he or she is love itself. There will be no person on this earth (exceptions are always

Love and Acceptance

there) who does not feel love or a need to cuddle a small baby. The infant is so innocent, pure, and so accepting that it attracts love from everyone, even a stranger. As the child grows to maturity, that innocence, that purity, that love—all fade away and everything for him or her becomes conditional. "If this, then that, if you then me". A person's beliefs, self-image, and nature is completely conditioned not only by the near and dear ones, but also by the society. They learn to manipulate, to conceal, and become self-centred. They learn to love not all but only those who fulfil their needs. Love, which was their natural quality, now becomes conditional and limited to their own interests and pleasures. It no more flows naturally.

Human beings, as they grow, seek knowledge and information for their own sake. As people become more knowledgeable, they mostly become hard at heart, insensitive, emotionless and without values. There is no innocence, no simplicity, and no humility left in them. It has become a fashion of the day today to use the word "love" so casually. *"Love you!"*, *"I really love you"*, *"you are so special for me"*, *"I cannot live without you"* — it goes on and on. But we need to ask ourselves, from the core of our heart, do we really mean these words when we say them? Or we say them just for the sake of saying them, or maybe we have become habituated to say them.

Kabir says that when we do not feel internally, we should not wear a mask on our face, i.e., we should not pretend. We need to be genuine in our emotions and expressions.

प्रेम बिना नहिं भेश कुछ, नाहक करै सुवाढ़ ।
प्रेम बाद जब लग नही, सबै भेश बरबाद ।।

प्रेमभाव एक चाहिए, भेष अनेक बनाय ।
चाहे घर में वास कर, चाहे बन को जाए ।।

Kabir Das says that love is a divine feeling and it is and should be there in everyone's heart. When love is in the heart, no matter what role you play, it hardly matters—whether you are living as a family person or as a spiritual person in deep forest.

Love is a selfless feeling. It has nothing to do with knowledge, information, qualifications, caste, creed, status, country, logic, or reasoning. We cannot think and love at the same time. "I will love this person when they do so and so action . . . I will love this person because . . ." does not work. In love there is no place for "because", "if", "then", or such conditions. When love happens, it is there and it has to be there no matter what. To understand love, we need to understand *acceptance*, because where there is unconditional acceptance there is love—automatically.

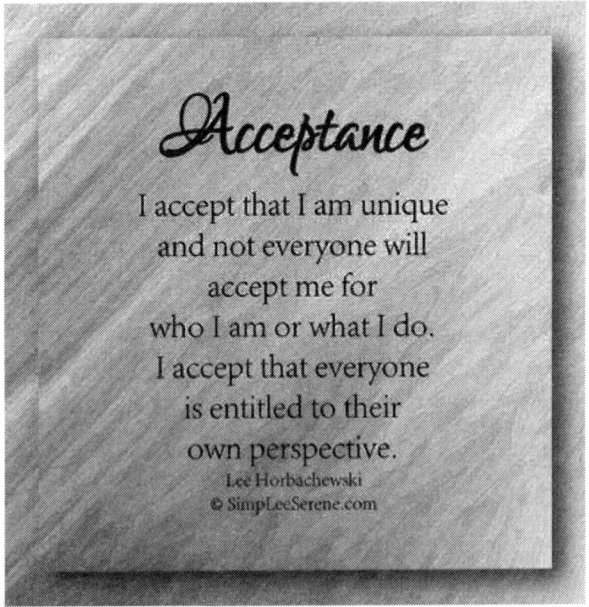

Kabir says that love is the need of every human being—to love and be loved. It is around this need itself that the world is revolving. Whatever we do (think for

Love and Acceptance

a minute and check for yourself) we do for acceptance (isn't it?), for recognition (isn't it?), for success (isn't it?), and all this for, ultimately, love. Somebody yearns for the love of parents, for the love of beloved and some might yearn for the love of God, for the Divine Power. Yes, there are people who love material things—car, houses, clothes, costly gifts—all for what? Just to satisfy the need for love and acceptance! We need to understand that this love is temporary. It is there today, might not be there tomorrow, but the love with our qualities, with our soul, and with the Divine Power is permanent. This love will always be there. We need to make our heart big, expand our aura and comfort zone, and learn to accept and love more and more people around us. Do it and see for yourself, you will feel so good, peaceful and satisfied!

प्रीती बहुत संसार में, नाना विधि की सोय।
उत्तम प्रीती सो जानियो, सतगुरु से जो होय।।

प्रेम-प्रेम सब कोइ कहैं, प्रेम न चीन्है कोय।
जा मारग साहिब मिलै, प्रेम कहावै सोय।।

In these two dohas Kabir Das says that there are many kinds and form of love in this world. However, love which is selfish, self-centred, and conditional is only temporary; it is only for a short while. True and real love is love with the Divine Power, because all other relationships are temporary and are merely attachments. When we love God truly, we are filled with good qualities for ever. Kabir also said that while everyone talks about love and the word is used loosely, but the predicament is that nobody understands its true meaning and sense. True love is that where we get an opportunity to realize ourselves, connect with ourselves in true sense, and gain true knowledge about God.

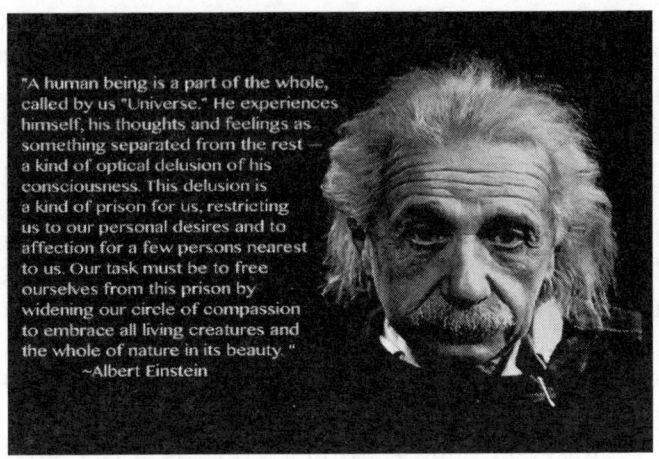

However, unfortunately, we look for faults in others:

दोस पराए देखि करि, चला हसन्त हसन्त।
अपने याद न आवई, जिनका आदि न अंत।।

Kabir says that it is human nature to laugh at and make a joke of others' faults and weaknesses, but we never try to look within ourselves and know our faults, which have no beginning and no end. Again, the fundamental principle is acceptance. When people do not accept themselves, do not love themselves, always project their own faults and weaknesses in others and so find faults in others, they keep criticizing, complaining, and condemning.

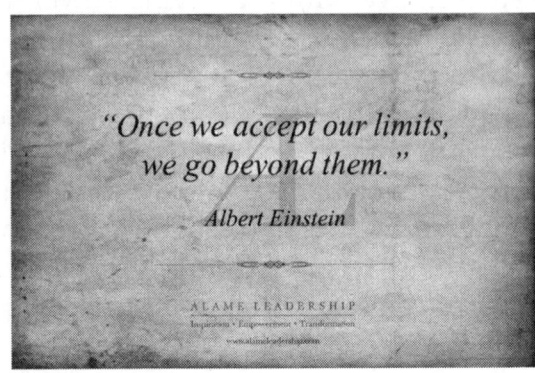

Love and Acceptance

Love is the most important characteristic of an emotionally intelligent person. IQ can only make you analytical, logical, and knowledgeable, but it is EQ (Emotional Quotient) or EI (Emotional Intelligence) that can help you to develop those soft qualities in you which make you a good human being.

पढ़ि पढ़ि के पत्थर भये, लिखि भये जुईट।
कबीर अन्तर प्रेम का, लागी नेक न छींट।।

Kabir says that people have become like stones by gaining more and more knowledge. They have become like rocks by just writing, i.e., they have become very hard like stones. They do not understand the real meaning of love. It is said that this is a knowledge world; there is no dearth of knowledge and everybody knows everything about everything. But they have lost the emotional part of their personality. They are no more simple, humble, and sensitive persons. In Freud's terms, their Id is too dominant and they seek only instant pleasure. That is the reason that crime and violence is increasing day by day. People want pleasure and instant gratification of their needs.

Pure and true love is always unconditional. It accepts the person as he or she is. It is non-judgemental. Love makes sacrifices. It always remains enthusiastic to help and offer support to the needy and to give them happiness. True love forgives and forgets.

धर्म किये धन ना घटे, नदी ना घटै नीर।
अपनी आंखों देखि ले, यो कथि कहहिं कबीर।।

Kabir says that a person's true goal in life is to serve others, be compassionate, and always keep doing good to others. This is true Dharma. Just like water does not decrease in a river and it keeps flowing, similarly if we keep doing good work continuously, our wealth will also never decrease. He says that we should do this for ourselves and see the results. It will surely happen—of course, the intentions must be pure.

> दया भाव हिरदै नही, ज्ञान कथै बेहद ।
> ते नर नरकहि जाहिंगे, सुनि सुनि साखी भाबद ॥

Kabir Das emphasizes that persons who do not have compassion in their heart or an intention for service to others, keep boasting of their knowledge. Such people just speak softly for formality and such people would definitely face lot of pain in future. For the well being of self and others, it is absolutely important to have compassionate feelings in our heart.

Love has many forms—compassion, sympathy, service, sacrifice, *mamta*, but forgiveness is the highest form of love. It is really very difficult to forgive, but whoever does it, attains divinity for sure. In Gita also, Lord Krishna said that by forgiving others we forgive ourselves and attain peace of mind. Unless we forgive others we constantly suffer from guilt, fear, and doubt, the three deadly emotions in human life. All these three emotions lead to lack of confidence and low self-esteem, and ultimately to all the negative emotions including irritation, anger, anxiety, fear, jealousy, etc.

> **Forgiveness is the best form of love. It takes a strong person to say sorry and an even stronger person to forgive.**
> ~Unknown
> 16quotes.com

Nobody can remain happy, peaceful, and satisfied without love and forgiveness. We need to remember that anger is a secondary emotion. Behind anger there is a hurt. When we are been hurt by some or the other person or by our own negativity, we feel angry. We need to heal that hurt. It is we who will do that. *Let us heal ourselves. Let us forgive ourselves. Let us forgive those who have hurt us. The persons who always forgive are truly Emotionally Intelligent.* They are not weak, as it may be thought for those who forgive and forget. They are the strongest. Weak are those who cannot forgive and who keep brooding and getting irritated and frustrated. They are actually weak because they have no control over their emotions.

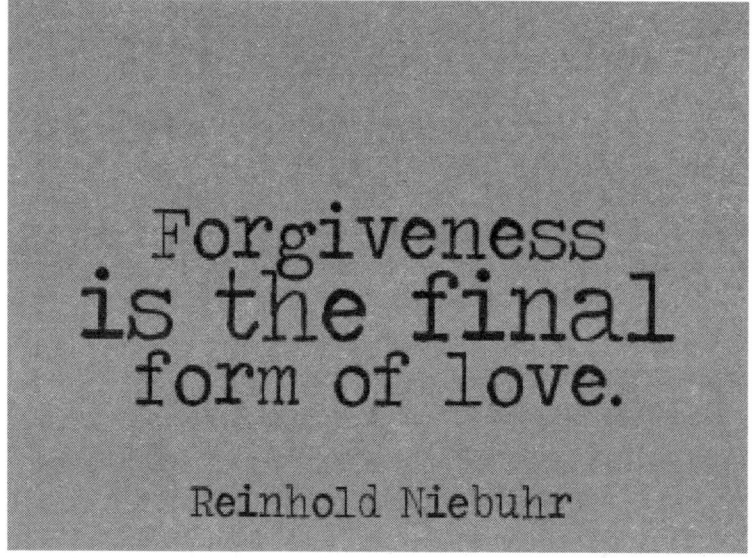

One of the important components of Emotional Intelligence is *self-regulation or self-management*. So if we are able to manage our emotions and regulate them in a positive direction, we are emotionally intelligent. Self-regulation or self-management is the second of the three key areas of personal skills that make up Emotional Intelligence. Self-regulation is concerned with how you control and manage yourself and your emotions, inner resources, and abilities. It also includes your ability to manage your impulses. Emotional intelligence suggests that it's important to be aware of all our emotions. When we're aware we can choose how to react and express our feelings. Self regulation is about using self awareness to keep negative reactions under control.

आवत गारी एक है, उलटन होय अनेक।
कह कबीर नहिं उलिटये, वही एक की एक।।

Here Kabir Das stresses that we should not react. If a person abuses us we should not react by abusing the person in return because then it holds double negativity. He says that instead of reacting, we should be calm, tolerate, and ignore. It will reduce all negativity and bring end to all bickering. An important life skill that makes a person emotionally strong is *anger management*. We have to learn to respond rather than react.

Anger management is a term used to describe the skills you need to recognise that you, or someone else, is becoming angry and take appropriate action to deal with the situation in a positive way. Anger management does not mean internalising or suppressing anger.

CONTROLLING YOUR ANGER

Anger is like fire. It can be a useful tool, or it can be hideously destructive. Certain situations require an immediate response, as when you witness some type of abuse or bullying, be it physical or psychological. But in other cases, smaller things could cause your anger to build up to the point at which you're in danger of losing control of your emotions. If you feel that's happening to you, try the following:

1. Leave

If you're in the middle of an extremely uncomfortable situation, it's difficult to not say the first thing that comes to mind. Before doing or saying something that you'll surely regret, get yourself away from the situation.

2. Take a few minutes to breathe deeply

According to the American Psychological Association (APA), deep breathing is one of the fastest ways to reduce the intensity of your anger.

Repeating a word or phrase that is calming to you (such as "relax," "let it go," or "take it easy") can also help soothe angry feelings.

3. Immerse yourself in something you enjoy

Once you take a break from the situation, look to engage in something that will divert your attention and help you calm down. Try reading, listening to music, or some other activity you find relaxing.

4. Try non-strenuous exercise

Go for a walk, a bike ride, or do some stretching. This can relieve the tension in your muscles and help you relax.

Putting it All Together

All of us will get angry from time to time. But using these strategies will help you to increase your EQ, control your anger, and express your feelings in a way that is more beneficial to you, and to others.[18]

---

18. http://www.inc.com/justin-bariso/how-emotionally-intelligent-people-deal-with-anger.html(accessed on 06 March 2017).

There are so many relationships that we are living every day. Parent-child relationship, husband-wife relationship, relationship with friends, teacher-taught relationship, employer-employee, daughter-in-law and mother-in-law relationship, and so on. There is no doubt about the fact that divorce rates are increasing day by day. Children and adolescents are facing problems and pressures from their parents and at schools and colleges and are facing cut-throat competitions. Suicide rates are on the rise. Each one of us has an innate need to control others. We want that others should do as we want them to do; they should behave, think, and act as we want them to behave, think, and act. We fail to understand why the other person is insisting on his or her point of view. If the other person goes or does anything against our wishes and desires, it hurts our ego and that creates conflicts in relationships. I think this is the story of every family!

Very few people understand that they can easily adjust and take care of other's feelings and emotions. You can feel such positive vibrations around them, in their

Love and Acceptance

house, in their relationships—whether it is husband-wife relationship or parent-child relationship.

> Remember, the way we treat others is the only thing that matters in eternity, and it impacts our prayers on earth. So today, choose love, choose forgiveness, and choose to treat others with respect so that your prayers can be powerful and effective the way God promises!

Emotionally intelligent persons are positive and optimistic persons. They see everything with a positive approach. They always send positive signals to people around them. They always try to see good things even in bad situations. They believe in themselves and in their God. They do not engage in unreasonable worry and anxiety. They are architects of their own fate, maker of their own destiny.

कबिरा क्या मै चिंतऊ, मन चिंते क्या होय।
मेरी चिंता हरि करे, चिंता मोहि न कोय॥

Kabir stressed that a person who has complete faith in God does not worry about anything. He also said that all pains and suffering are due to expectations. Once this expectation is over, there is no space left for fear or worry. Mind becomes free from attachment and gains peace. The person becomes happy—the ultimate goal of their life.

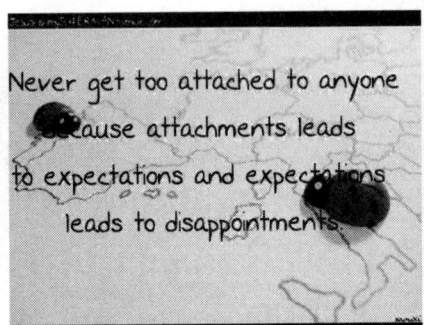

Where is the sensitivity? Isn't it dying each day? This positive quality in the language that is much in vogue today is Emotional Intelligence. With decades of experience of doing without it, humans have come to the conclusion that there is something missing in their life—something which helps them function better in all spheres of life, from their career to their personal life, that can help a kid and can equally help an elderly person in making a decision. And to acquire that something, we do not need to cram any more text books or answer difficult viva voce examinations, but rely on a sound gut feeling, something that ought to come naturally to us but has been curtailed and restricted by decades of teaching and conditioning. Now is the time to think with our heart, for the heart feels!

कबीरा गर्व ना कीजिये, काल गहे कर केश।
और ना जाने कित मारना, का घर का परदेश।।

कबीर गर्व न कीजिए, रंक न हसिए कोए।
अजहूं नाव समुद्र में, ना जानौ क्या होय।।

In the words of Kabir, we should not feel egoistic about anything, for example, our body, strength, caste, etc. Nor should we laugh at the weak and make fun of

Love and Acceptance

them. He says that our own lives are in the midst of a deep ocean. Nobody knows what will happen in the very next moment.

Kabir Das also says that we should not be proud of anything, as death holds everyone by their hair. No one knows when it will take our life and where it will kill us. So we need to be humble and down to earth and not boast of our strengths and achievements. The letter *I* is a symbol of ownership and possessiveness. It is self-centred and not at all concerned about the feelings and emotions. When *I* dominates, we lose our decision making and problem solving ability because then only negative emotions dominate us and our minds. It is a paradoxical world. It is very strange that a person, when he or she achieves great heights and reaches the top of their career, they become very rigid, egoistic, and then *ahankaar* dominates. Here I would like to quote lines from a famous ghazal, a very good example of narcissism (self-love):

> Khuda humko aisi khudai na de
> Ki apne siwa aur koi dikhai na de

Kabir says:

> जब मै था तब गुरु नहीं, अब गुरु है मैं नाहिं।
> प्रेम गली अति सांकरी, तामें दो न समांही।।

Kabir Das says that when our heart is filled with selfish interests and ego, it becomes difficult to realize God. Once God is realized and we get the blessings of a Guru, *ahankaar* leaves our heart and mind and we become a pure soul. The path of love is very narrow and both God and ego together cannot stay together. So when God is there in the heart, *ahankaar* cannot be present at all.

> We all are visitors on this earth. We came empty handed and will go empty handed, leaving all our efforts, creations, and relations back here. Only our karma will come with us to decide our future. Good karma gives a happy future and bad karma gives a painful future. Karma is the results of good and bad actions we performed during our life. Let us go with a basket of fruits of good karmas when we leave the earth.

Everyone wants to live an easy and happy life. To achieve it, we all work every day. Most of us put efforts for our entire life but never enjoy it as per desire. One day, life ends without notice and without achievement or satisfaction. This is true for most people.

Peace, happiness, and satisfaction come from balanced status of mind. If you look, you will realize that we get excited very quickly. Our mental tolerance level to favourable and unfavourable events is very low. With positive or favourable news, we react very joyously, but only for a short time. Happiness ends soon and we fall back to our regular cycle of work, responsibility, stress, desire, and anxiety. Our maximum life passes in this cycle.

Happiness or unhappiness is nothing but states of mind. They are mental reactions to any occurrence or occasion. Regular study and practice of the following keys will increase the mental power to react to any occurrence or occasion in a balanced way. These keys are made to open the door of our life to long term happiness.[19]

---

19. http://www.thepeace.org/golden_keys/golden_keys.html(accessed on 06 March 2017).

Key 1:
I am just a visitor here. We all are visitors here.
We all came on this earth for a temporary period and eventually will go. We all are just visitors.

Key 2:
We all will go alone and empty handed.
Nobody can carry anything from this world. Everyone will go alone leaving all of his/her relations, creations, business, wealth and even their own bodies. If nothing comes together, then why should we waste in our whole life for accumulation and creations of wealth and power which are not going to come with us?

Key 3:
Our desire and needs are endless, but life has an end.
Do not waste this life running behind new desires. Remember, everyday arising desires and needs never get fulfilled completely and life ends, suddenly. Our life is shorter than we realize. Control the needs and desires and pass the valuable life with ease and less burden of fulfilment. Remember, happier is *not* the one who has more, but it is the one who needs less.

Key 4:
Today will not come back and tomorrow is not guaranteed.
Enjoy the passing moments of life without waiting for tomorrow. Do not spoil moments of the current life in the hope of an uncertain tomorrow. Do not wait for big happiness to happen, instead find and enjoy every day's small happiness.

Key 5:
Nothing lasts for ever.
Good or bad things, memories, situations, and events settle to normal as time passes by. Time heals the

wounds. Health, wealth, power and relation of a person, enterprise or nation changes the phase over the time. Nothing lasts for ever.

Key 6:
Enjoy what you already have.
Most of us do not enjoy what we have because of desire of getting more and more. We never enjoy our life in this cycle of chase. Leave this chase. Relax and look around for many small enjoyments awaiting your attention.

Key 7:
Remember everyone's help in your growth.
You will find a lot of help extended in your growth, from birth to your current level. Never forget all invaluable and selfless love, affection, care and support you received from your parents, relatives, and friends during various stages of your life. Also, never step back to extend your help and care to them when they are in need.

Key 8:
What you give to others, you will get back the same in plenty.
This is the law of God and it applies to all living beings. God is always watching everyone invisibly and very quietly. "He" is taking notes on our each action and thinking. Accordingly, we get reward or punishment in some way. Always be helpful to *all* lives, including all creatures. If you want to be happy, keep others happy. If you want peace, give others peace. Remember, some day your action will bounce back to you, with more force.

Key 9:
Grab an opportunity of being helpful.
Whenever you get the opportunity of being helpful to anyone, do not lose it. Be helpful to needy people by physical assistance, by mental support, or by monetary help. Create a habit to assist. This habit will give you great satisfaction, mental peace and keep you away from unhealthy stress, greed, and anger. You are also shaping your happy future by helping others.

Key 10:
Keep regular touch of a good lesson.
Good reading is healthy food for the mind. Give your mind this healthy food every day for some time. Good reading or listening every day for a few minutes gives mental peace and keeps your life cycle on the right track. Remember, a peaceful mind creates peace in the family.

Key 11:
Eat non violent food for peaceful and healthy living.
Our body is very complicated but a perfect machine. It needs energy to work efficiently. This energy comes from our diet. We should feed our body in a punctual way with a healthy diet. Frequent over and irregular eating is not good for our health. Foods high in cholesterol or fat (like animal and dairy products) create health hazards like ulcers, cancer, and heart attacks. Avoid such food. Use more vegetables in the diet. A vegetarian diet is perfect for the human body for a healthy and long life.

Key 12:
Leave bad and unhealthy habits.
To live a long and healthy life, leave hazardous habits like smoking and alcohol. Go to sleep on time and wake

up early. Plan some relaxed time with all family members every day. A happy family is that which stays together, prays together, and eats together.

REALIZATIONS

1. An emotionally intelligent person loves and accepts himself or herself and others unconditionally. Human beings do not become intelligent by reading heavy books or by becoming too qualified, but by feeling love for others and accepting others as they are.
2. Love is the basic nature of humans; it is a selfless feeling and the need of everyone.
3. Unfortunately, humans have become egoistic and self-centred. We only loves ourselves and blame, criticize, condemn, and complains about others. We do not accept others, finds faults in them, and draws sadistic pleasure out of it.
4. Love is an important characteristic of an emotionally intelligent person. Forgiveness is the highest form of love. The person who forgives is not weak; rather, he or she is a very strong person.
5. Human beings suffer from three deadly emotions—guilt, fear, and doubt. All these three emotions lead to lack of confidence, low self-esteem, and ultimately to all negative emotions.
6. We should shed our ego and develop humility.

Fifth Realization

Connection with the Self and the Divine: Power of Satisfaction

Connection with the Self and the Divine: Power of Satisfaction

Human beings have become selfish to a great extent. We only want and seek our own comfort and our own security. We also want more love for ourselves. We takes life for granted and forget the Divine Power when we are satisfied, happy, and when things are moving according to our desires and will. It is only when we face some problems in life or some discomfort that we look up to the God and asks for forgiveness and help. Kabir Das says that humans should give up this selfishness, this *ahankaar*, egoism and remember God more in our happy days. If we do so, we will feel more empowered and powerful to face the challenges of life in a much more positive way.

जब मैं था तब हरी नहीं, अब हरी है मैं नाही।
सब अँधियारा मिट गया, दीपक देखा माही।।

We call ourselves educated, literate, knowledgeable, intellectual, wise people, but for what and for whom? This is a very pertinent question each one of us should ask ourselves. This knowledge is making people egoistic, greedy, murderers, corrupt, and self-centred individuals. This is a very paradoxical world. With all my humble respect and acceptance of the religious groups and modern saints, what I experience is that most of the people who are more into all these satsangs, religious groups, and spiritual sermons are more disturbed, anxious, hyperactive, insecure, and of dual personality. What a predicament! Such people should be calm and relaxed, taking things in their stride. But unfortunately, they are not. Why? Then what's the use of these satsangs?

Connection with the Self and the Divine: Power of Satisfaction

Kabir said in this doha that when *I* dominates the existence of an individual, the person becomes egoistic and the darkness of *ahankaar* envelopes the person. But as soon as the Guru or the teacher provides knowledge, enlightens the person with their wisdom, this darkness vanishes and the person can see the reality. In the light of this knowledge, Kabir says we can find the ultimate— God. But, there is this big but, that means that the words of the Guru will also work and have an effect only when our heart, mind, and thoughts are pure and receptive. Just listening, blindly following the Guru, but not changing our thoughts and remaining shrewd and negative from inside will not enlighten us in any and neither can we get close to God.

साधु भया तो क्या भया, बोले नाहि विचारि।
हते पराई आत्मा, जीभ बाधि तलवारि।।

Here Kabir Das said that people who take up the spiritual path, there is nothing great about it if the person does not think before he speaks. If their words hurt the emotions of others, what is the use of their being spiritual or following God's path?

माला फेरत जुग भया, फिरा न मन का फेर।
कर का मनका डार दे, मन का मनका फेर।।

Kabir Das says that some people keep chanting, using a *mala*, for years and years, but there is no change in their thoughts, feelings, or perception. They do not understand the real meaning of truth and love. Such people should stop posing as *sants* and *mahatmas* and work on changing their thoughts and follow the path of truth, love, and compassion in the real sense. It is only when they understand their thoughts intelligently that they can be called emotionally intelligent.

> Only through our connectedness to others can we really know and enhance the self. And only through working on the self can we begin to enhance our connectedness to others.
>
> Harriet Lerner
> meetville.com

निरबंधन बंधा रहे, बंधा निरबंध होय।
कर्म करै करता नहीं, निरबंध कहावै सोय॥

मन मुआ माया मुई, संशय मुआ भारीर।
अविनाशी जो ना मरे, तो क्या मरे कबीर॥

Kabir Das says that all those sants and mahatmas who wear a mask of a sadhu but have no control on their senses and who keep thinking of internal and external pleasures, such people are actually bound in chains rather than free. Only such a person is free in real sense who, although engaged in the worldly affairs, lives a simple life without wearing any mask and who has control on all the senses. Only such a person is a real *karmyogi* who simply believes in doing the duty and is free in the real sense.

Kabir Das says that a person who has controlled his *maan*, attachments, desires and has killed his *ahankaar* and ego becomes free from the cycle of birth and death and then does not fear death at all.

This doha was written and is being studied for the last hundreds of years. But doesn't it seem more correct in the present scenario and in the present context? Yes, surely! The more an individual is educated and qualified, the more he or she is losing their values, wisdom, understanding, and decision making power and becoming more and more egoistic. People are being influenced so much by the media and technology that they have stopped using their wisdom to differentiate between right and wrong. What use is such education if we are not able to make our children and youth emotionally intelligent, understanding, and good human beings?

Kabir said that education will enlighten people and bring them more close to God for the larger benefit of the society and people. But it is a sorry fact that today education is not only taking people away from God but from their real self too. Everything in our life is centred on *I*. Seriously, we have not left even God in that. We consider ourselves the most sincere *bhakt* of God. "*Tere bhaktjano main humse badhkar kaun?*" We have become so selfish that we remember God only when we think that now it is only He who can help and save us.

दुःख में सुमिरन सब करे, सुख में करै न कोय।
जो सुख में सुमिरन करे, दुःख काहे को होय।।

It is not that a person who remembers God in good days will not face any problem in life. *Sukha* and *dukha* are two sides of the same coin, a part of life. We have to face both till the last breath of our lives. But the person who forgoes selfishness and remembers God equally in both *sukha* and *dukha*, will not get much anxious and worried in sad situations and will be able to face them more bravely.

Both *sukha* and *dukha* are a state of mind. They do not depend on any external source. It is our thoughts that make us either feel happy or depressed in any particular situation. If we analyse a little deeply, we will find that it is a habit of every human being to connect with people only at times of happiness or good times, but when bad times dawn on them, we run away from them.

दुःख लेने जावै नहीं, आवै आचा बूच।
सुख का पहरा होयगा, दुःख करेगा कूच।।

Kabir Das says that nobody stays near when we are sad or having difficult days. During bad days people run away, but when a person is having good and happy days everyone will come near. Yes, this is the truth of life! Humans have become very selfish in nature. We always look for our own interest and our own happiness.

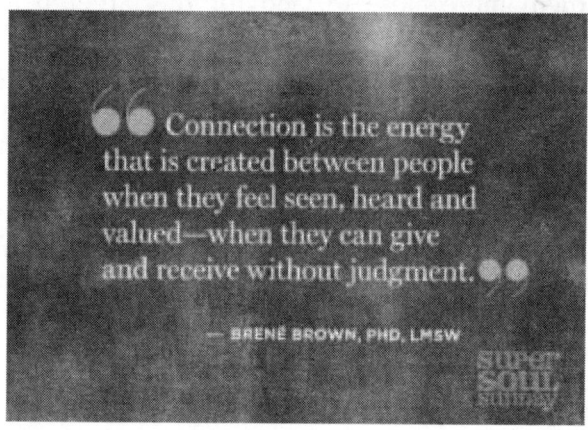

प्रभुता को सब कोऊ भजे, प्रभु को भजे ना कोये।
जो कबीर प्रभु को भजे, प्रभुता चेरी होये।।

Kabir Das says that people are running after name and fame, but they do not give importance nor remember the Divine Power through which they achieve this name and fame. Kabir stressed that if we pray to God, think of Him sincerely, and with full humility, name and fame will automatically come to us.

उदर समता अन्न ले, तनहि समात चीर।
अधिकहिं संग्रह ना करै, तिसका नाम फकीर।।

Connection with the Self and the Divine: Power of Satisfaction

Kabir Das says that a fakir (saint) is a person who takes food and clothes according to the need and who does not accumulate them beyond his needs. We are all immersed in greed and numerous desires and wants which are never satisfied. But a person who does not accumulate unreasonably, who remains satisfied with what he has, is a saint in the real sense. Satisfaction is a divine quality which helps us in connecting to the Almighty. We simply need to curb our desires by being aware and conscious. Whenever you feel the desire for anything new, just simply ask "Is it really required?" "Do I need it now?" If you get an answer in the negative, take a step back mentally and stop yourself from acquiring it.

साईं इतना दीजिये, जा मे कुटुम समाय।
मैं भी भूखा न रहूँ, साधु ना भूखा जाय।।

Here Kabir talks about *satisfaction* — another important parameter of a mentally healthy and emotionally intelligent person. Every human being is engaged in a rat race today. We all are running like mad persons; the predicament is that we do not know after or for what we are running. We all are upset because we feel that we do not have time — but time for what? It is an important question to ask ourselves. A few years ago life seemed so cool and relaxed. Why? It was because we did not have too many ambitions, too many engagements, too much competition. We were satisfied with what we had. We had peace of mind. But today we want more of everything. No doubt, each one of us is ultimately working and living for satisfaction, happiness, peace, and harmony, but are we satisfied at the end of the day? God has given everyone enough for their survival, but it is the greed of human beings to have more and more, which ultimately leads to dissatisfaction.

देख पराई चूपड़ी, क्यो ललचाए जी।
रूखी सूखी खाय के, ठंडा पानी पी।।

This means that we should not be jealous of others' happiness. We should be satisfied with whatever we have. Even if we have simple food to eat, we should be happy. We should eat it with satisfaction and drink cool water, rather than remaining jealous of others who have rich food to eat and other costly things with them. Thus, Kabir Das emphasizes that we need to be satisfied with whatever we have, because there is no end to desires and wants.

Greed mars the wisdom of a person and the person fails to distinguish between right and wrong.

कबीर औंधी खोपड़ी, कबहूं धापै नांहि।
तीन लोक की संपदा, कब आवै घर मांहि।।

Humans are never satisfied with wealth and physical amenities. Their desires and needs keep on increasing day and night. A greedy person keeps thinking how he or she can attain the wealth of all three realms of the world. Such persons are too attached to their wealth and property. For them, their richness, wealth, and property are their life and nothing else.

बहुत जतन करि कीजिये, सब फल जाय नशाय।
कबीर संचय सूम धन, अंत चोर ले जाय।।

Kabir also emphasized the importance of "giving" or *daan*. He says that we all have enough to be able to satisfy and give to the needy; we should have the heart and the courage to give. We should not be a miser because, ultimately, all this wealth will be destroyed and nothing will go with us. From Emotional Intelligence point of view, mentally healthy persons are satisfied with themselves and their situations. They are those who can easily adjust and not compromise with their situations.

Kabir Das explains that we need to curb our desires and wants. The less we desire and expect, the more our life would be simple and satisfied. There is always a negative correlation between greed and satisfaction. The more the greed, less the satisfaction. More the desires, more you remain stressed and depressed. It is also true that more the desires and expectations, more the person is ready to forego their values and morals for the satisfaction of those desires.

Kabir Das also stressed that we should not feel proud about what we have because what we have today might not be with us tomorrow. Big houses, branded clothes, big and chauffeur driven cars—all these material things give pleasure and comfort just for a few days, then you stop drawing any pleasure from them and they become old. They can provide us comfort, but not happiness. Our happiness has become conditional and depends on these material things. Kabir says:

कबीर गर्ब न कीजिये, ऊँचा देखि अवास।
काल परौं भुंइ लेटना, ऊपर जमसी घास।।

कबीर जोदिन आज है, सोदिन नहीं काल।
चेति सकै तो चेत ले, मीच परी है ख्याल।।

एक दिन ऐसा होयगा, सबसों परै बिछोह।
राजा राना राव एक, सावधान क्यों नहिं होय।।

गौधन, गजधन, बाजधन, और रतनधन खान।
जब आए संतोश धन, सब धन धूलि समान।।

In all these dohas, Kabir stresses the importance of satisfaction as an important quality. This is also the characteristic of an emotionally healthy and intelligent person. Satisfaction is a pure and divine quality of an emotionally intelligent person that takes a person nearer to God. A satisfied person has peace of mind and more concentration in his or her work. Kabir says that even after attaining all the wealth of the world—gold, silver, cows, elephants, horses, precious stones, etc., a person is not satisfied. But when he or she achieves satisfaction and ultimate peace of mind, they find that all the wealth is like dust. After attaining satisfaction, they achieves ultimate happiness. We achieve satisfaction when we learn to have complete control on our desires and needs. Wise people, who do not give in to the desires of their mind (*maan*), but use their intellect (*buddhi*) to understand the need and importance of those desires, are emotionally intelligent in the real sense. Just think, we always say, "*hamara maan kar raha hai, ye lene ka, ye paane ka.*" Do we ever say, "*hamari buddhi keh rahi hai ye lena hai, ye paana hai*"? It is basically our mind (*maan*) which dominates us and we give in so easily to the desires of our mind because it is seeking pleasure every moment. We have to empower ourselves to control our mind to brighten and enlighten our intellect so that, before we try to fulfil any need, we use our intellect and our logic to decide.

सदा रहैं संतोष में, धरम आप दृढ़ धार।
आस एक गुरूदेव की, और न चित्त विचार।।

Those who have understood the importance of satisfaction gain happiness for whole life. Saints and people on the spiritual path are completely satisfied. They are not anxious or desirous of anything in this world. They just aim for the realization of God and have no worldly thoughts and desires in their heart.

चाह गई चिंता मिटी, मनुआं बेपरवाह।
जिसको कछु न चाहिये, सोई साहंसाह।।

Connection with the Self and the Divine: Power of Satisfaction

The cause of all the worries of human beings are their unlimited desires and expectations. When we control our desires, we control our anxiety and worry and our mind becomes free.

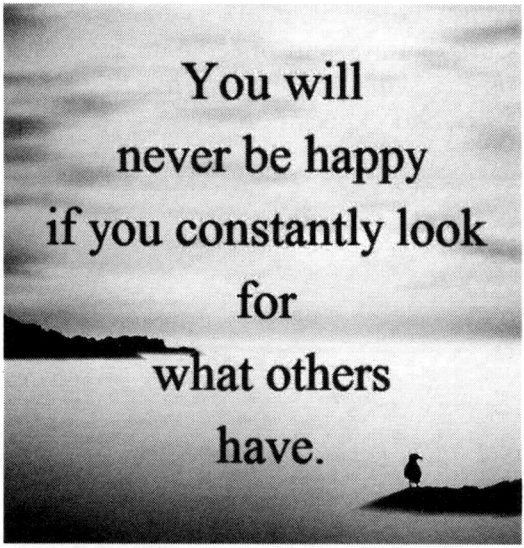

You will never be happy if you constantly look for what others have.

It is hard to be satisfied with life, if you're never satisfied with yourself.

WWW.LIVELIFEHAPPY.COM

With no desires, the heart and mind become happy. Swami Vivekananda also said that there is no end to desires. When one desire is fulfilled, we look forward to another and so the list of unlimited desires goes on and on. We hope that after achieving a particular thing we will gain happiness, but the predicament is that it gives pleasure for few hours or days and once again we find ourselves standing on the same platform, trying to achieve or fulfil another desire and expectation.

We become servants of our desires. The desires start dominating us. We become weak emotionally. If one desire is not fulfilled we become depressed, anxious, and start having sleepless nights in expectation of fulfilling our desires. These endless desires create hurdles in a human's ultimate goal of life, that is to achieve *moksha*.

Connection with the Self and the Divine: Power of Satisfaction

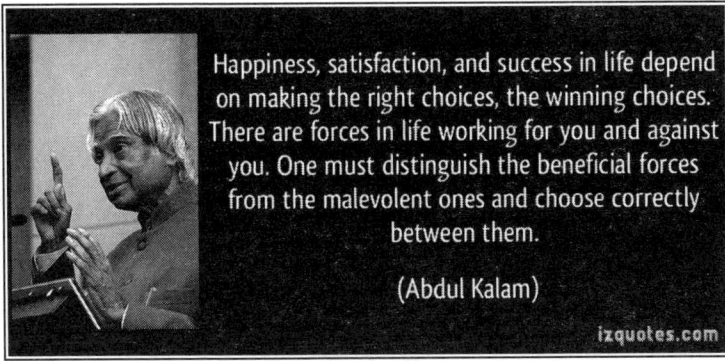

Happiness, satisfaction, and success in life depend on making the right choices, the winning choices. There are forces in life working for you and against you. One must distinguish the beneficial forces from the malevolent ones and choose correctly between them.

(Abdul Kalam)

Bhagwad Gita and Swami Vivekananda both emphasize the fact that it is not possible for a human being to give up all his or her desires and expectations. So the best way is to keep doing our duty in this world and not desire the fruits of this duty. *Karm karen phal ki icha na rakhen.* In very simple language, it means to do our duty and keep no or minimum expectations from the people around us. Because where there is expectation, there is frustration; there is stress, anxiety and depression.

Realizations

1. Humans have become too selfish and seek their own comfort and security.
2. Human beings remember God only in their time of sorrow and forget Him in their happy days.
3. When ahankaar dominates, even a Guru cannot change the mind of the ahankaari person. People should stop posing as satsangis if they have no control on their greed and negative thoughts and behaviour.
4. A person who can control his maan, attachments, desires, and can control his or her ego, becomes free from the cycle of birth and death and is also free from the fear of death.
5. Sukha and dukha are states of mind.
6. Satisfaction is another important parameter of a mentally healthy and emotionally intelligent person. It is a divine quality of a person. We should curb our desires and wants and develop the quality of giving.

Sixth Realization

Connecting Sweetly: The Power of Effective Communication and Humility

Connecting Sweetly: The Power of Effective Communication and Humility

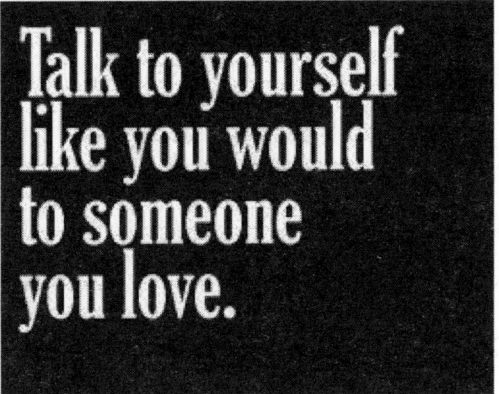

ऐसी बानी बोलिये, मन का आपा खोय।
औरन को शीतल करै, आपौ शीतल होय।।

People face relationship oriented problems and these problems basically arise due to lack of proper communication and criticism of one another. It is very easy to point out the negative side of a person; it is rare that people focus on the positive characteristics of the other person. They try to bring into focus their own positive qualities and put the other person down. They taunt, criticize, condemn, and complain. All this ultimately brings negativity in any relationship. Kabir Das, through this doha, emphasizes that we should shirk our ego, *ahankaar* and speak such a language and in such a loving tone that it not only makes the other person feel happy and good, but it also makes ourselves feel peaceful at heart. It is through language and communication that we connect with each other and our language and communication should be as sweet as possible.

It is human nature to find fault in others and to blame others. We fail to see our own faults and imperfections. Kabir says:

> बुरा जो देखन मै चला, बुरा न मिलिया कोय।
> जो मन ढूंढ़ा आपना, मुझसा बुरा ना कोय॥
>
> करे बुराई सुख चहै, कैसे पावै कोय।
> बोए पेड़ बबूल का, आम कहां ते होय॥

A person who is strong physically, socially, and financially, starts thinking about himself or herself to be God. They consider themselves to be all powerful and thinks that they can overpower the weak. But at the end, they are the one who stand empty handed, all alone, absolutely lonely, with no relations, no satisfaction, no happiness, and no peace of mind.

In the above two dohas, Kabir Das says that when I went out to find to look for a bad person, I was surprised that there was no one worse than myself. In this world, everyone, because of their false ego, *ahankaar*, consider themselves to be good and absolutely right, but the person who, with full humility, does self-analysis and tries to ponder over his or her own strengths and weaknesses, can find and work upon the weaknesses. Kabir also says that after doing a bad act, if we expect something good in return, it is our foolishness. Just like when we foolishly expect sweetness of a mango from the tree of acacia (babool). Only when a person is good from heart and their thoughts and actions, can they smell like a flower and spill their fragrance all around. Otherwise, by being bad and always remaining busy in shrewd thoughts and acts, we cannot for maintain for very long our cleverness. One day, for sure, we will be disliked by people around us.

जो तोको कांटा बुवै, ताहि बुवै तू फूल।
तेहि फूल को फूल हैं, वाको है तिरशूल।।

Kabir Das thus emphasizes that we should always be good to others even if the other person harms us or sows thorns for us. If we sow flowers for them, we too will get flowers in return. We have to be patient. Thus, no matter to what extent people are bad with us, try to harm us, we should always be good to them.

I understand that while reading this, many of you might be facing conflict in this principle and must be thinking that if somebody is being rude to you, is thinking bad for you, how can we be good in return? But, dear friends, if you really want to see the effect of good actions on your side, you have to do it; may be once, twice or a number of times, you might not get any result, but for sure, one day the person will get tired and will fall at your feet, will ask for forgiveness. If you are good, don't give up your forgiveness for someone who is bad.

An emotionally intelligent person not only speaks positively with other persons, but also has listening power. Communication is a two way process. If we only speak, with our mind closed to what other person wants to say or express, then that is not true communication. And this is what happens often in any and every relationship around us. We want people to agree with whatever we tell them without questioning, without any argument, because *I* have said so. Again, that *I* dominates. We do not want to accept the other person's point of view, what he or she feels or thinks about the issue.

कुटिल वचन सबतें बुरा, जारि करै सब छार।
साधु वचन जल रूप है, बरसै अमृत धार।।

मधुर वचन है औषधि, कुटिल वचन है तीर।
श्रवन द्वार है संचरे, साले सकल सरीर।।

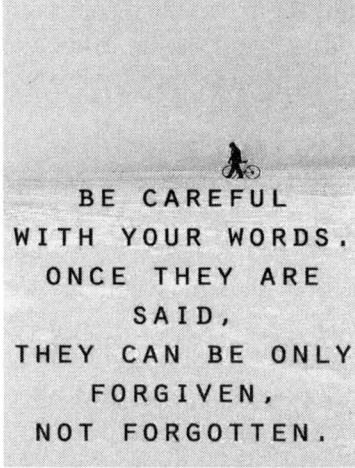

Kabir Das also emphasizes that words have great power. How these words can affect the personality of an individual, we cannot simply imagine. Moreover, words have different influence on different people. Therefore, we should always think before we speak and utter our words. Anything said politely and lovingly acts as a medicine, whereas harsh words hurt a person just like an arrow. We have to speak truth, but politely. Many problems are created by misuse of words. So we must use sweet, polite, and proper words, suitable to the occasion. Our words also reveal our personality.

शब्द सहारे बोलिये, शब्द के हाथ न पाव।
एक शब्द औषिधि करे, एक शब्द करे घाव।।

बोली एक अनमोल है, जो कोई बोलै जानि।
हिये तराजू तौलि के, तब मुख बाहर आनि।।

Kabir Das emphasizes that we should always think and weigh our words before we speak it to someone. He says it is very important to speak carefully and choose our words properly before we speak, because words do not have hands and feet, but words do have many forms.

Some words might act like medicine and might have healing power; on the other hand, some other words might hurt the person and might give him or her sorrow and make them feel low. He also says that:

अति का भला न बोलना, अति की भली न चूप।
अति का भला न बरसना, अति की भली न धूप।।

This doha says that it is neither good to speak too much nor to be silent too much. Just as too much of rain and too much of sunlight is not good. This means that our words have great power. We should always think before we speak and wisely understand the situation where we need to be silent and contemplate (consider) the situation.

> **If we understood the power of our thoughts, we would guard them more closely. If we understood the awesome power of our words, we would prefer silence to almost anything negative. In our thoughts and words we create our own weaknesses and our own strengths.**
>
> ~ Betty Eadie ~

बालू जैसी किरकिरी, ऊजल जैसी धूप।
ऐसी मीठी कदु नहीं, जैसी मीठी चूप।।

वद विवादे विश घना, बोले बहुत उपाध।
मौनि गहै सबकी सहै, सुमिरै नाम अगाध।।

The saint says that no other object has the grittiness of sand. Also, nothing has the bright light of the sun. Similarly, nothing is sweeter than silence. Kabir says that remaining silent is a great auspicious act that is practised by sadhus and sants.

While reading, it seems that there is a contradiction with the previous doha, where Kabir Das has said that too much of silence is not good. However, there are situations in our lives when we need to remain quiet at that particular moment and not get into an argument. When the situation is under control, we should always speak up.

Kabir says that arguments are like poison. They have no end but definitely have the power to hurt the feelings of others and kill relationships. It is because of arguments and negative words that people become enemies of one another, leading to unhappiness and unrest. Even Dale Carnegie, one of the greatest motivational speakers, said, "The best way to get out of an argument is to avoid it."

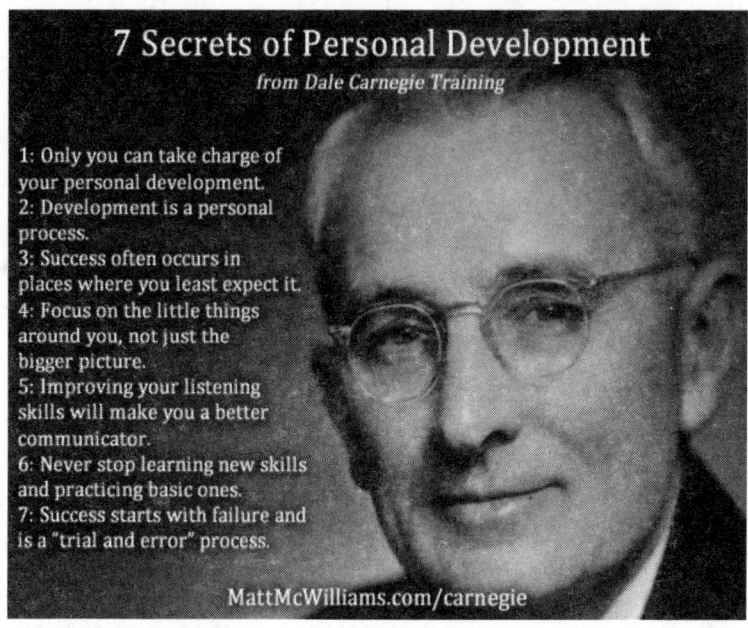

The messages, whether positive or negative, that we give other people every moment have a powerful influence on their self-esteem. These messages, either boost up their self-esteem and confidence or demoralize them and break and hurt their existence. For example, if someone tells us that we are a nice person, or we have done a wonderful job, or we work hard, and care so much for other people, how are we going to feel? *Good, collars up,* isn't it?

On the other hand, if every moment we have to listen to messages like "you are good for nothing", "you will not be able to do it", "you cannot do anything", and about how we look, how we talk, etc., what will be our feeling? Of course, we will feel low, depressed, feel lack of confidence, and above all, we start feeling the same, i.e., we start living the messages that we are given—*a self-fulfilling prophecy*. (A *self-fulfilling prophecy* is a prediction that directly or indirectly causes itself to become true, by the very terms of the prophecy itself, due to positive feedback between belief and behaviour.)

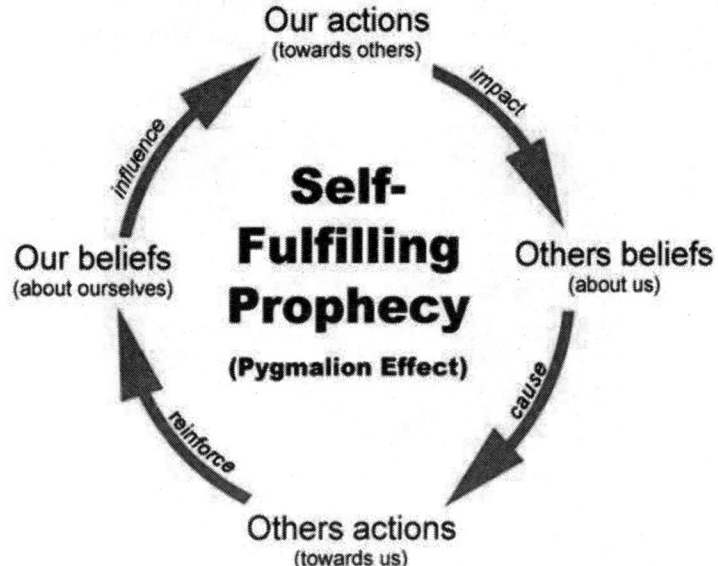

There is a difference between *acceptance* and *approval*. If we understand this difference, we can form healthy, positive relationships. It is not necessary that we approve of or agree with what the other person says or thinks, but we should appreciate his or her point of view because whatever the other person thinks or feels, it is on the basis of their experiences, past or present, and it cannot be wrong. So we should learn to understand what others say. Once we understand, it becomes easy to explain our point of view to the other person in a positive manner. We can tell them, "Yes, I accept what you say, I understand your point of view, but I think and feel like . . ." and so the communication takes place in a positive direction, with no bickering or arguments. This is how people become receptive. Humans' nature, their feelings, thoughts, and beliefs are formed through their experiences in life, and so whatever they believe, cannot be right or wrong because it is based on their experiences.

Kabir Das explains that we should sacrifice or give away the feeling of *ahankaar* in our hearts. We should be humble and speak simple and sweet words to others so that it not only gives coolness and calmness to their hearts, but also gives peace and harmony to our own selves.

जिह्वा में अमृत बसै, जो कोई जानै बोल।
विश वासुकि का उतरे, जिह्वा तनै हिलोल।।

शीलवंत सबसे बड़ा, सब रतनन की खान।
तीन लोक की संपदा, रही शील में आन।।

Kabir tell us that humility and humbleness is the greatest quality of a person. It is like a mine or an umbrella that embraces all other qualities. Even if a person has all the wealth of the world, he or she can gain respect only if they are humble and speak sweetly and lovingly. Also, a person who has knowledge or is aware about the importance of words, knows that sweet words act as honey and shower peace and happiness. By speaking sweet words, with all humbleness, respect, and love, we can even win the heart of an egoistic person and he, too, can become humble, just like the poison of a poisonous snake goes down by speaking sweet words from the tongue.

Thus, if we internalize and follow this simple doha that we should speak positive language and in a loving tone that brings peace to the other person, we can win people's hearts and expand our aura. We need to understand that people love and respect those who are polite and cultured. A humble and courteous person keeps others happy, takes care of others' needs and tries his or her best not to hurt others through his or her emotions and actions.

If we ponder over the fact that while God has given us two ears, but only one tongue, we will realise that it is His intention that we use our ears more and our tongue less. Before we speak, we must think whether our words are likely to hurt the listener. Anything that hurts us is likely to hurt others, too. So, if words spoken to us are likely to hurt us, we must not speak them to others. Those who gossip may speak a thousand words in the course of a day, but a *jnani* (a wise person) may speak only a few. But the few words of the *jnani* are more pregnant with meaning than the many words of an ordinary gossiping person.

We must not be angry when elders advise us, even if their words of advice are a little harsh. Will a plant grow in the shade? No, it needs sunlight. The sun's heat is scorching, and yet the plant needs sunlight to thrive. In the same way, the words of those who wish us ill may be comforting, but they are like the shade in which nothing grows. But the words of *jnanis*, even if they might not be pleasant to us, will benefit us in the long run.

ज्ञानी अभिमानी नहीं, सब काहू सो हेत।
सत्यवान परमार थी, आदर भाव सहेत।।

In this doha Kabir Das stressed that a wise and a learned person is never egoistic or arrogant. They always keep thinking about the welfare of others and always behave lovingly towards others. They always follow the path of truth and believe in inculcating divine qualities in themselves. From Emotional Intelligence point of view also, the meaning of this doha relates very well to an important quality and characteristic of an emotionally intelligent person. As mentioned earlier, emotionally intelligent persons believe in maintaining healthy relationships with people around them. They are aware about their own emotions and those of others, are sensitive and can empathize with others' pain and pleasures. Emotionally intelligent persons always try their best not to hurt others' feelings by speaking harsh words. Also, they are never egoistic and takes care of others' needs and feelings.

कागा कोका धन हरै, कोयल काको देत।
मीठा शब्द सुनाय के, जग अपनो करि लेत।।

In this doha Kabir says that a crow never snatches the wealth of anybody, nor a cuckoo gives anything to anyone, but her sweet and melodious voice is liked by everyone and delights people everywhere. By speaking sweetly and in a melodious and loving tone, we can also bring the whole world in our aura and comfort zone. Do it and see it for yourself. It definitely works!

One who talks sweetly does not have an enemy and is blessed with plenty of wealth and good fortune.

– Rig Veda

REALIZATIONS

1. People mostly face relationship oriented problems and these problems basically arise due to lack of proper communication and criticism of one another.
2. An Emotionally Intelligent person not only speaks positively with other persons but also has a listening power.
3. Communication is a two-way process.
4. Thoughts and words have great power and affect the personality of an individual. Anything said politely and lovingly acts as a medicine, whereas harsh words hurt like an arrow. The messages have a powerful influence on the self-esteem of a person.
5. Humility is not a weakness. Rather, being humble and courteous requires power and strength which all do not have. A humble and courteous person keeps others happy, takes care of others needs and tries his or her best not to hurt the feelings of others through his or her emotions and actions.

Seventh Realization

Healthy Relationships

Healthy Relationships

जग में बैरी कोई नहीं, जो मन शीतल होय।
यह आपा तो डाल दे, दया करे सब कोय।।

Emotional Intelligence explains that we should remain happy, good, and caring towards people. Kabir Das says that if our mind and heart are at peace, no one can become our enemy or have negative feelings for us. He says that if we give away our ego, our *ahankaar*, and can transform this ego into humility, compassion, and affection, people will start liking us, praising us, and we will be loved by one and all.

We have all experienced at some time in our lives that if we are genuinely concerned about the other person and give him or her respect, show care and concern towards that person, appreciate him or her, then that person is always good towards us in any gathering anywhere. Yes, exceptions are always there, but in most cases the person is getting some benefit from us and for that he or she shows us his humbleness and respects us (flattering us). It is a well known and experienced fact that if we are good to people, a large number of people connect to us because we are constantly sending positive signals to them. Our aura and comfort zone expands and more and more people like to connect with us. On the other hand, if we are arrogant, aggressive, and irritated every time, brooding every time and have ego (*ahankaar*), nobody wants to talk to us or be with us for a long time. Therefore, what Kabir Das said so many years ago in this couplet is explained in the concept of Emotional Intelligence.

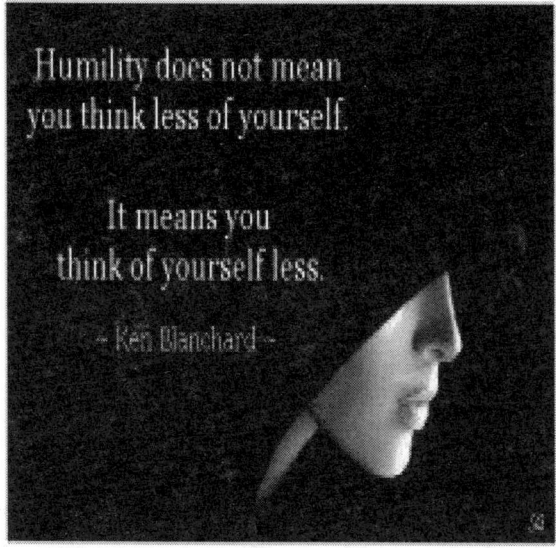

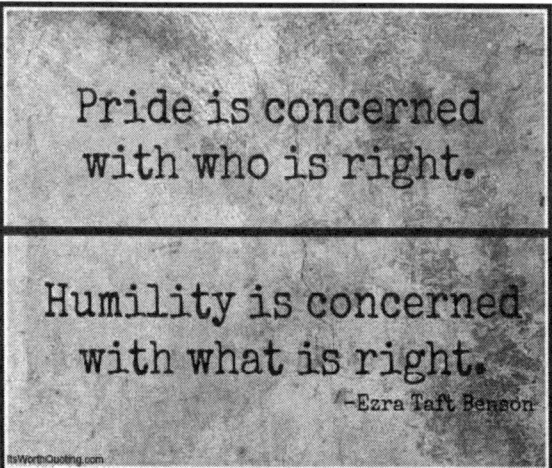

We need to inculcate the value of forgiveness in us if we want to maintain healthy and positive relationships—*forgive and forget*. There are people who, for years, keep thinking and criticizing the person who somehow how has hurt them or done anything wrong to them. They are not able to forgive them and move ahead. Forgiving the other person is the most challenging and important quality of an emotionally intelligent person. A person who forgives is a great soul. He or she is strong not weak because they have the courage to overlook the wrong that is done to them. Instead of criticizing the person at fault, we should try our best to empower them to transform themselves so that they can become good human beings who will never commit that mistake again and thus we can help them to grow in life.

Generally, on a daily basis, we actually demoralize, humiliate, and embarrass the person who commits a mistake. We use statements like *"tum bahut murkh ho"*, *"tumse koi kaam nahi hota"*, *"zindgi main kya kar paoge jab itna sa kaam nahi hota* and so on goes the list of messages that we give people every day. Such messages/ somewhere or the other, break and hurt the existence of the person.

जहाँ दया तहाँ धर्म है, जहाँ लोभ तहाँ पाप।
जहाँ क्रोध तहाँ पाप है, जहाँ क्षमा तहाँ आप॥

Kabir says that where there is compassion, there is Dharma; where there is greed, there is sin; where there is anger, there is death; and where there is forgiveness, there is God, real self, the pure soul. There is no point in keeping the conflicts and bickering in our heart for a long time. For what? Who is being hurt more? Obviously, the person who gets irritated and angry every minute of his or her life, because of someone else and not the person who is actually wrong. How does it matter to him or her?

Humans are considered to be the best creation of God. There is absolutely no doubt about it. It is also a universal fact that humans are social animals. Humans cannot survive without other people. The predicament is that when humans are not faithful with God, their creator, then what to talk of their faithfulness in their relationships. Humans have really become so greedy, so selfish. Let us ask this important question from ourselves — Do I want this relationship with this person because I get so and so from him or her? It is sad to see that we have become so conditional in our relationships with other people. Every time and in every relationship we are thinking of our own interests and satisfaction and take other people for granted. We are creating negative energy in our hearts. Just imagine, we make our heart weak with this negative energy. All negative emotions and feelings—revenge, greed, anger, irritation, jealousy, hatred and other such feelings create negative energy and produce harmful hormones in our body due to which we fall prey to a number of physical ailments. Research has proved that today almost all the physical diseases are psychosomatic, i.e., physical diseases with psychological reasons. Diseases like diabetes, thyroid, blood pressure, allergies, tumours, migraines, etc., all have psychological reasons. The more stress you have, the more such diseases start building in you.

Psychosomatic Disorders

- Psychosomatic disorders (i.e. those that involve physical symptoms, but have an emotional or psychological origin)
- Psoriasis, eczema, stomach ulcers, high blood pressure, and heart disease have all be shown to be triggered and exacerbated by psychological factors, such as stress and anxiety
- In the West, the prevalence of psychosomatic diseases continues to increase in line with stress in our social environment

Love is complete only with forgiveness and forgiveness comes with acceptance. When we forgive, we rise rather than fall; when we forgive and says sorry, it means that we consider the relationship more important than the issue, consider the person more important than the particular thing over which the conflict took place.

Anger is a very natural emotion. It is an expression of the feeling of hurt, frustration, or dissatisfaction. Just think and analyze the last when you were angry and what had actually happened. You were angry because you were hurt and frustrated (was it so?). So we need to work on our feelings of hurt and frustration and heal ourselves. Thus the anger will vanish.

कोटि करम लागे रहै, एक क्रोध की लार।
किया कराया सब गया, जब आया हंकार।।

Kabir Das says that anger is simply one emotion, but it has many other negative feelings attached with it like jealousy, greed, and attachments that emanate from possessiveness. When a person becomes angry, all his or her good actions go waste and are destroyed.

Emotional Intelligence is when we can understand our emotions as much as we can understand the other person's emotions. For that we need to see things from the other person's point of view. When we can stand in the other person's shoes and see the world through his or her eyes, that is Emotional Intelligence. And such understanding will definitely help us maintain our relationships life long, in a healthy manner.

Kabir Das always talked of other people's welfare. He always advised to look within ourselves. First analyse ourselves, our strengths and weaknesses. It is only when we accept himself or herself that we will be able to accept the other person with all his or her weaknesses and negativities.

बुरा जो देखन मैं चला, बुरा न मिलिया कोय।
जो दिल खोजा आपना, मुझसे बुरा न कोय।।

Nothing is good or bad, thinking makes it so. As our thoughts, so we see the world. If we are good at heart, always think about the welfare of the other people, take care of the emotions of other people, always check our tone, our language, we will always send positive vibrations around us. Thus everyone will seem nice to us, good to us and everything will look beautiful. We always have some negative people around us who always brood and talk nothing but negative. They start their day with a brooding face and always complain and criticize. An emotionally intelligent person is a happy person, satisfied person, adjusting, and a positive person.

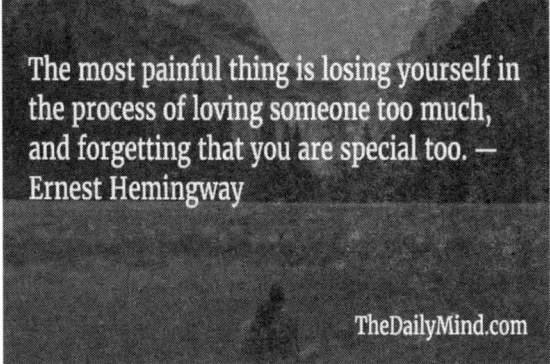

The most painful thing is losing yourself in the process of loving someone too much, and forgetting that you are special too. — Ernest Hemingway

TheDailyMind.com

Realizations

1. *Forgive and forget is an important principle for a healthy relationship.*
2. *Three Natural Laws are important for a healthy and positive relationship. They are accept, appreciate, and adjust.*
3. *"Adjust" is a positive word and not negative. Its negative connotation is to compromise, where you submit yourself, your desires, and feelings to the wishes of others. But "adjust" is a positive word—you maintain a balance with likes and dislikes of others.*
4. *Emotional Intelligence is when we can stand in the other person's shoes and see the world through his or her eyes.*
5. *An Emotionally Intelligent person is a happy, satisfied, adjusting, and appositive person and does not take relations for granted and a means to fulfil his or her own interests.*

Eighth Realization

Don't Worry, Be Happy!

Don't Worry, Be Happy!

> **"Worrying doesn't take away tomorrow's troubles. It takes away today's joy.**
> ~ Anonymous ~

People have a habit of constantly worrying. They worry and become stressed on trivial, i.e., unreasonable matters. In today's world, a majority of the physical problems that people face is related to stress. Even very young children are becoming physically diseased due to stress and mental pressure.

चिंता ऐसी डाकिनी, काटि करेजा खाए।
वैद्य बिचारा क्या करे, कहां तक दवा खवाय।।

Kabir has also stressed on worry and peace. He says that worrying is a habit and this habit takes away all peace from a person's life. No doctor has any medicine for this disease. A person who has developed this habit of constant worrying cannot remain peaceful nor can he or she be positive in thoughts and feelings. Such a person always thinks negatively about everything. "If this happens, then?", "If he does not come back, then?", "If I will not get that, then?? There is always a doubt in the person's mind. If? Then? Worrying is about future, the future which is unpredictable. But such a person, on the basis of false assumptions, sees the future and that too all negative. *And we need to understand that whatever we think, it eventually happens*. If we are constantly thinking negatively, negative things happen with us. We cannot get to any solution of our problems by worrying. Worrying clouds our mind with negative emotions and diminishes our power to think solutions to the problem. To get to the right solution, we need to be peaceful, calm, and quiet. And this is possible only when we are thinking correctly and positively.

As I have discussed earlier in the book, our mind or *maan* is always trying to fool us. It never lets us win or remain committed to our promises. Let us consider an example. How many of us want to get up early in morning, say at 4 a.m. and how many of us are able to get up at that time? Very few, isn't it? As soon as the alarm rings, our mind asks us to stop it and tells us to go off to sleep just a little more—only to get up finally at 7 a.m. "*Dekha jayega jo hoga*", "*abhi uthte hain*", "*thoda aur so len*". Does it not happen with most of us? Why? It is because our mind dominates our intellect. We are weak. We are not able to overpower the desires of our mind or *maan*.

मन चलता तन भी चलै, ताते मन को घेर।
तनम न दोऊ बसि करै, होय राई सुमेर॥

There should be a harmony between mind and body and this is possible only through yoga and meditation.

तन थिर मन थिर वचन थिर, सरति निरति थिर होय।
कहैं कबीर उस पलक को, कल्प न पावै कोय॥

Kabir Das says that when our body is stable, mind is stable, mind is at peace, and when words are also in our control, then all negativities also become peaceful and settle down. At that moment, we become stable in our real self and come to terms with our original nature. Overall, Kabir Das emphasizes that we should be calm and quiet in our mind, body, and thoughts. Then all negative emotions will be in control.

मन मोटा मन पातरा, मन पानी मन लाय।
मन के जैसी ऊपजै, तैसे ही हवै जाय।।

In the above doha, Kabir Das stresses that the mind, i.e., *maan*, sometimes becomes strong and sometimes seems so weak and simple. Sometimes it is so cool and calm like water and at other times it is furious like a fire. Thus, the mind takes the shape of the quality of our thoughts; as our thoughts so our mind and *maan*.

मन पंखी बिन पंख का, जहां तहां उड़ि जाय।
मन भावे ताको मिले, घट में आन समाय।।

Our mind is a free bird, without wings. But still, even without wings, it keeps flying here and there. It very easily gets influenced by whoever it meets and takes its shape and form. This means that our mind is very unstable and it cannot remain at one place. So Kabir Das teaches us to control our mind and our thoughts.

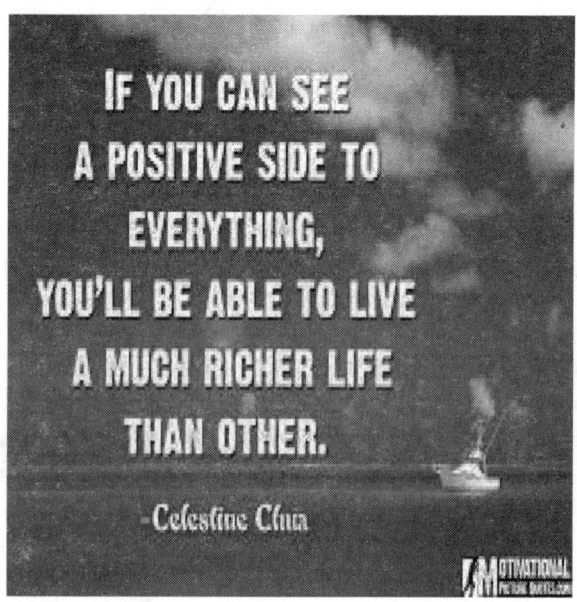

Don't Worry, Be Happy!

Worry is, sadly, an inevitability of life. Bad things are bound to happen, and the natural human reaction is to think about the negative consequences that could potentially arise. However, worry is rarely productive—"it's something we do over and over again, without much resolution, and it's typically of the worst-case scenario of the future," explains Jason Moser, Ph.D., an assistant professor in the Department of Psychology at Michigan State University, who has conducted studies on worry.

> **STOP Worrying About:**
> Things outside of your control.
> Things that won't matter a week/month/year from today. Why waste today worrying?
> What people think of you right now, you can change their minds later.
> What could have been. Stay open for what's next.
> Pleasing others all the time, it's not selfish to focus on yourself every now and then.
> selfstairway.com

We should learn to talk positively. Words have immense power. *You can try this here and now*!

For a few minutes, keep telling yourself and feel, "I am having severe headache." Remember, speak and feel at the same time that you are having a severe headache. What will happen? You will start feeling and probably start having a headache. The holy Gita also stresses *"Kyon vyarth chinta karte ho"*. Things on which we do not have control, we should not worry about and leave everything to God. Have faith on Him. We say this, but do we believe in these words? Our problem is that we don't believe what we say. We say we have faith in God, but do we really have that faith in times of problems or stress?

चातुर को चिंता घनी, नहिं मूरख को लाज।
सर अवसर जानै नहीं, पेट भरन सूं काज।।

Kabir Das says that a person who has the goal in life to realize and see God, who is curious to attain the Divine love, and is thoughtful, need not worry much to improve his behaviour because God will Himself take care of him. However, people who are ignorant, fools, who do not realize the love of God, do not feel ashamed about it. They are comfort loving people; they just eat, sleep, and go away from this world. They are not goal oriented people and are like animals.

Peace is a state of mind that can be achieved. It is the absence of worry, fear, anxiety, and irritation. It is a balanced state. Kabir Das says that we should have faith in God and after that we should not worry about anything. Those who do not believe in any existence of Divine power should have faith on themselves and their capacities. Emotional Intelligence also stresses that accepting ourselves and having faith on ourselves and our potential can lead to the solution of every problem, big or small.

Thus happiness, peace and satisfaction are states of mind. They are perspectives, approaches to view things in life. If we see things in right and positive perspective and with a positive approach, our mind and heart will remain peaceful, satisfied, and happy and vice versa. Some of us think that happiness is something that will come in future—it is kept there, quite far off—and when we reach there, then we will get happiness.

Till now, right from our childhood, we have always been talking and emphasizing on IQ, i.e., cognitive intelligence. But now its high time for every one of us to understand that peace within and peace in the society at large can be achieved, not when people become more

Don't Worry, Be Happy! 97

knowledgeable and cognitively intelligent, but only when they develop Emotional Intelligence (EI). This EI can be developed only by working on important aspects of our personality and life skills like self-regulation, self-motivation, empathy, and social and interpersonal skills. It is only when we work on these skills that we can become emotionally mature and strong. Simple life principles need to be understood and internalized (*inhe atmasaat karna hai*) and followed. For example, smile often; do not criticize, condemn, or complain; keep clear and open communication in any and every relationship; stop worrying about trivial matters; try to be sensitive to other person's needs; love more, understand more, and feel more; be positive—the list goes and on. Remember, these principles are not just to be read but to be followed every day and then see the results. It definitely helps!

As I have already said earlier, people usually face relationship oriented problems. There is a need to get more connected in relationships. We have become more digitalized rather than sensitized; more connected to internet rather than Inner Net. We use WhatsApp, Facebook, and other such means of communication with our loved ones and friends instead of preferring to sit face to face and have a real communication. We use smileys to express our emotions. For example, if angry, a smiley showing teeth; if we want to hug and love, we a show smiley with a red colour kiss. Yes?

If we want to smile, smileys with a curved line smile.

Is this how we express our emotions face to face? No!

There is a need to get more connected with people. This is not attachment I am talking about, but we should be good, empathetic, and humble. Kabir Das said in his doha:

प्रीत रीत सब अर्थ की, परमारथ की नाहिं।
कहैं कबीर परमारथी, बिरला कोई कलि माहिं।।

He says that in the present world, people have become selfish, self-centred, and do not care much about what other person feels or thinks or how much he or she gets hurt by their behaviour. It is very rare to find people who are unselfish, detached and peacefully do their duty for which God has sent them. Kabir says:

धन रहै न जोबन रहै, रहै न गांव न ठांव।
कबीर जग मे जस रहे, करिदे किसी का काम।।

He says that nothing will remain with us ultimately—neither wealth, nor house, nor beauty, not anything else. Therefore, we should always remember this reality and keep doing good to others and think of their welfare. This is the characteristic of an emotionally intelligent person. At this point, I also remember beautiful lines of Robert Frost:

> The woods are lovely, dark and deep,
> But I have promises to keep,
> And miles to go before I sleep,
> And miles to go before I sleep.

> राजपाट धन पायके, क्यों करता अभिमान।
> पड़ोसी की जो दशा, सो अपनी जान।।

Kabir Das says that there is no use in feeling proud about the wealth and property that we have. It is all false and a means of giving sorrow. Death is the ultimate reality. We all have to die one day and all this wealth and property will remain here. It will not go with us. So, why do we feel so proud? Kabir Das also says:

> आय हैं सो जाएँगे, राजा रंक फकीर।
> एक सिंहासन चढ़ी चले, एक बँधे जात जंजीर।।

Whoever has taken birth in this world is definitely going to die, whether he is rich or poor. It is all God's *maya* that one gets all the wealth and the other is bound by chains of caste and creed. And so, from Emotional Intelligence point of view also, we should learn to accept the reality of birth and death and understand that God has sent us to this world to be happy, to make others happy, to serve others, and always work for their welfare.

The famous song from film *Pyasa* of Guru Dutt also enlightens us about the reality of this life that no person is happy and satisfied. Everyone is sad, anxious, and depressed somewhere or the other. Although it is a song with a negative tone, if we try to imbibe its positivity, we realize that it says that *ye duniya agar mil bhi jaye to kya hai*, meaning thereby that real happiness and satisfaction is not in relationships and material things, but in having true and loving relationship with your own real self and with the Almighty.

Yeh mehlon, yeh takhton, yeh taajon ki duniya
Yeh insaan ke dushman samaajon ki duniya
Yeh daulat key bhookhey rawajon ki duniya
Yeh duniya agar mil bhi jaaye to kya hai
Yeh duniya agar mil bhi jaaye to kya hai

Har ek jism ghayal, har ek rooh pyaasi
Nigahon mein uljhan, dilon mein udaasi
Yeh duniya hai ya aalam-e-badhawasi
Yeh duniya agar mil bhi jaye to kya hai

Yahaan ik khilona hai insaan ki hasti
Yeh basti hai murda paraston ki basti
Yahaan to jeevan sey hai maut sasti
Yeh duniya agar mil bhi jaye to kya hai

Yeh duniya jahaan aadmi kuch nahi hai
Wafa kuch nahi, dosti kuch nahi hai
Yahaan pyaar ki qadr hi kuch nahi hai
Yeh duniya agar mil bhi jaye to kya hai

REALIZATIONS

1. *The major physical problems today are related to stress and worry.*
2. *Worrying is a habit and is based on false assumptions.*
3. *Happiness, peace, and satisfaction are states of mind.*
4. *Today human beings are becoming more digitalized than sensitized.*
5. *Nothing is permanent in this world. So we should be satisfied with what we have and bring peace and harmony to our mind.*
6. *We should keep ourselves busy in positive things and should not worry about minor issues.*
7. *We need to live in the present rather than brood about the past and worry about the unknown future.*

Ninth Realization

Emotional Intelligence and Well Being: The Power of Positive Attitude

Emotional Intelligence and Well Being: The Power of Positive Attitude

People who are emotionally healthy are in control of their emotions and their behaviour. They are able to handle life's challenges, build strong relationships, and recover from setbacks. But just as it requires effort to build or maintain physical health, so it is with mental and emotional health. Improving our emotional health can be a rewarding experience, benefiting all aspects of your life, including boosting our mood, building resilience (flexibility), and adding to our overall enjoyment of life. Being emotionally and mentally healthy doesn't mean never going through bad times or experiencing emotional problems. We all go through disappointments, loss, and change. And while these are normal parts of life, they can still cause sadness, anxiety, and stress.

The difference is that people with good emotional health have an ability to bounce back from adversity, trauma, and stress. This ability is called *resilience*. People who are emotionally and mentally healthy have the tools for coping with difficult situations and maintaining a positive outlook. They remain focused, flexible, and creative in bad times as well as good. One of the key factors in resilience is the ability to balance stress and our emotions. The capacity to recognize our emotions and express them appropriately helps us avoid getting stuck in depression, anxiety, or other negative mood states. Another key factor is having a strong support network. Having trusted people we can turn to for encouragement and support, will boost our resilience in tough times.[20]

---

20. www.ithembacc.org.za/articles/emotional-and-mental-wellbeing/9 (accessed on 10 April, 2017).

People who are emotionally and mentally healthy have:
1. A sense of contentment.
2. An enthusiasm for living and ability to laugh.
3. The ability to handle stress and bounce back from adversity.
4. A sense of meaning and purpose in life.
5. A balance between work and play, rest and activity.
6. The flexibility to learn new things and adjust to change.
7. The ability to build and maintain fulfilling relationships.
8. Self confidence and high self esteem.

No matter how much time we devote to improving our mental and emotional health, we will still need the company of others to feel and be our best. Humans are social creatures with an emotional need for relationships and positive connections with others. We're not meant to survive, let alone thrive, in isolation. Our social brains crave companionship—even when experience has made us shy and distrustful of others.

Social interaction—specifically, talking to someone else about our problems—can also help to reduce stress. The key is to find a supportive relationship with someone who is a "good listener"—someone we can talk to regularly, preferably face-to-face, who will listen to us without a pre-existing agenda for how we should think or feel. A good listener will listen to the feelings behind our words, and won't interrupt or judge or criticize us. The best way is to find a good listener. But first be a good listener ourselves. We should develop a friendship with someone we can talk to regularly, and then listen and support each other.

Mental health is how we think, feel, and act as we face life's situations. It is how we look at ourselves, our lives, and the people in our lives. It is how we evaluate options and make choices. Like our physical health, our mental health is important at every stage of life. Mental health includes how we handle stress, relate to others, and make decisions. Mental health ranges from good to not so good and even to poor. A person's mental health may move through the range; sometimes that person is healthier than at other times. Sometimes he or she needs help in handling problems. Many people experience mental health problems at some time during their lives. Mental health can impact the daily life and the future of a young person. For example, schoolwork, relationships, and physical health can be affected by mental health.

Mental health may be better understood by its comparison with physical health. A person is said to be physically healthy when his or her body is functioning well and he or she is free from pains and troubles. Similarly, a person is in good mental health when his or her mind or personality is functioning effectively and he or she is free from emotional disturbances. In general the persons enjoys life and any unhappiness they have can be understandably explained. They are self-confident, hopeful about themselves and their opportunities though they may have temporary setbacks and discouragements. They have a few intimate and close friends, maintain cordial relations with a number of people whom he meets and generally gets along with all those with whom they come in contact in life and work. They are able to meet their problems without much disturbance, and their fears and anxieties are normal. They keep a composed temper and when aroused expresses their anger in a socially acceptable way. They are concerned about their health, but not hyper-anxious about it. They have emotional maturity, balance, and equilibrium. They not only understand themselves, their merits and abilities, their handicaps and disabilities, but also accept them and makes the most of their mental and physical capacity.

Mentally healthy and emotionally intelligent persons live in the present rather than brooding about the past and worrying about the future. We need to understand that the past is dead and gone. It will never come back. The only thing that we can get from our past is to learn from the mistakes that we have done. But it is really sad to know that there are a number of people who keep brooding and crying about what happened in the past. They live their life filled with guilt and fear—guilt about the mistakes that have been committed by them in the past and fear of rejection by their loved ones. Fifty per cent of people doubt their future. What will happen? Whether it will happen or not? When will it happen? So on and so forth. They are never satisfied and simply keep worrying about the future—future which is unknown and unpredictable.

People fail to understand that it is only "the present" that is there in our hands—yes, only this moment. When a person is reading this book, only this moment is there in his or her hands, which will instantly become a past moment. Time is the most powerful factor in a human being's life and the most neglected one by everyone. We take time for granted and try to control it according to our own needs and desires. Kabir Das, in the following doha, emphasizes:

काल करे सो आज कर, आज करे सो अब।
पल में प्रलय होएगी, बहुरि करेगा कब।।

He stressed that instead of wasting time and procrastinating (*talna*) your work for tomorrow, we should complete it today and instead of leaving it for the end of the day, it should be done now, because this is the very moment that is in our hand. Who has seen the evening or the next morning? Thus, Kabir says that instead of finding causes for not doing the work, instead of procrastinating and postponing for other day or some other time, and instead of being lazy, we should build enthusiasm in our heart and mind and finish off the work here and now. This is also an important life skill—time management.

Kabir said:
चले गए सो ना मिले, किसको पूंछूं बात।
मात पिता सुत बांधवा, झूठा सब संघात।।

Kabir said that death is the only reality of life. Many have gone and the rest who are existing will definitely go. Parents, sibling, children, and every other relation is just an attachment and a false perception. Everyone will leave us. Even we will leave this life one day. Hence, we need to accept the reality, move ahead in life, and fulfil our duties.

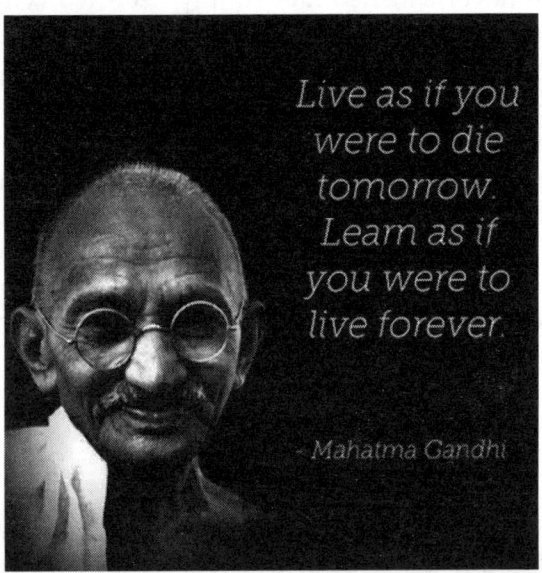

> "Even death is not to be feared by one who has lived wisely"
> Buddha
> CarolynAndersonMD.com

The best indicator of an emotionally intelligent and healthy person is his or her positive attitude towards life. He or she understand the importance of life, time, and relationships. They understand that this life is unique, given by God and they make their greatest effort to make the most of their lives.

रात गंवाई सोय के, दिवस गंवाया खाय।
हीरा जन्म अनमोल था, कोड़ी बदले जाय।।

Kabir Das emphasizes that negative people lose their life by just sleeping in the night and eating during the day. This life, which is valuable like a diamond, is lost like something unimportant. This doha of Kabir, written so many years ago, is still relevant in the present times. Through this doha, I want to appeal the youth of my country to become conscious and stop wasting their unique life and time in irrelevant and meaningless things. As I have mentioned earlier also, most of the time of our youth is wasted in WhatsApp, Facebook, and such social networking sites, using mobiles, and watching T.V., partying, visiting discos, and other such activities. This young generation is the future of the country. It is important for them to become aware and conscious and start using the precious and valuable moments of their lives in some constructive and positive activities so that they can contribute to the benefit of the society and the world at large.

कबीर यह तन जात है, सकै तो ठौर लगाव।
कै सेवा कर साधु की, कै गुरु के गुन गाव।।

दुर्लभ मानुष जन्म है, देह न बारम्बार।
तरुवर ज्यों पत्ती झड़े, बहुरिन लागे डार।।

Kabir Das stresses that this human life is unique and valuable. It is unique among all the species created by the Almighty. We need to realize the fact that time is flying too fast and every day we are wasting these valuable moments of life. When the end will come, we don't know which moment will be our last moment; we will not get this human life again and again. So do not waste it. We should now become conscious and do something good for our own welfare and the welfare of others. This is Emotional Intelligence in the real sense—to be conscious and understanding and become wise.

बहुत जतन करि कीजिये, सब फल जाय नसाय।
कबीर संचै सूम धन, अंत चोर लै जाये।।

Kabir says that all the wealth collected with great efforts will go waste and get destroyed if it is not used for others. Misers never give anything to anybody and believe in accumulating wealth and assets. But unfortunately, at the end, they have nothing in hand and everyone of us have to die empty handed. Kabir says that our wisdom and divine quality is proved by our compassion, when we are always ready to give.

Kabir emphasizes that humans are never satisfied. Humans always want more and more. A greedy person keeps thinking how he or she can earn more and more by hook or by crook. Whatever they achieve, there is no end to their greed and desires. Kabir also emphasizes that there is a relationship between greed and attachment. A greedy person loves only his or her money. For them, nothing is more important than money.

जब मन लागा लोभ सों, गया विशय में भोय।
कहैं कबीर विचारि के, केहि प्रकार धन होय।।

Kabir says that when a person gets completely involved in making money and becomes greedy, then he or she has nothing else to think about day and night except how they can earn more and more money by hook or by crook. Such persons always remain thirsty for name, fame, money, property, and materialistic things and gets never satisfied.

> To live is not sufficient. We need also the joy of living; and the joy of life requires health. Above all we need that health which embraces body, mind and soul.
>
> – *Alexic Carrel*

We need to understand this in terms of Emotional intelligence that satisfaction is one of the most important factors for a healthy mind and body, and for a healthy soul too. Satisfaction is the foundation of a mentally healthy person. When a person is satisfied he or she is peaceful and in harmony. Only then can there be a balance in his or her thoughts, feelings, and actions. Thoughts are important. What and how we think influences our feelings and finally it affects our behaviour. For example, if we say to ourselves, "*I am good for nothing*" or "*main kisi kaam ka nahi hun*" or "*mujhse kuch nahi hoga*", and so on, how will we feel when we give ourselves these messages and thoughts? Of course, we do not feel good. We feel lonely, depressed, demoralized and our self-esteem goes down. Now how does it show in our behaviour? Firstly, whatever we do, we do not do it enthusiastically; we approach everything negatively. We lose confidence; we get nervous, cannot communicate properly, become passive, stop having eye contact with people while talking, and also start feeling weak physically and mentally.

Now see the opposite—a picture of persons who are satisfied, peaceful, and happy with what they have. They are positive persons with a positive approach to things. They always send positive signals to everyone around. They have a larger comfort zone and aura as compared to negative persons. These persons are very confident, accept themselves as they are, and also accept other people with all their strengths and weaknesses. They see good and positive in every aspect of life. They communicate effectively in an assertive manner and know how to listen. They can empathize with people and understand their problems and situations. They are satisfied persons, happy and peaceful and in harmony with all the aspects of their lives and personality.

सदा रहैं संतोष में, धरम आप दृढ़ धार।
आस एक गुरूदेव की, और न चित्त विचार।।

Kabir Das, in this doha, states that good people and positive people are not dissatisfied. They accept their religion and religious practices with determination. Their ultimate purpose of life is to connect and unite with the Ultimate. They have neither attachments, nor expectations, nor any worldly thoughts in their hearts and minds. I would like to quote a line of a famous bhajan of Shri Hari Om Sharan:

Man maila aur tan ko dhoye
phool ko chahe kante boye

kare dikhava bhakti ka tu ujli odhe chadariya
bhitar se man saaf kiya na bahar manje gagariya
parmeshwar nit dwar pe aaya tu bhola raha soye
kabhi na man mandir mein tune prem ki jyot jalayi

sukha paane tu dar dar bhatke janam hua dukhdayi
ab bhi naam sumir le hari ka janam vritha kyu khoye

swanson ka anmol khajana din din lutata jaye
moti lene aaya tat pe seep se man behlaaye
saancha sukha to paye sharan prabhu ki hoye

Kabir says:

तन को जोगी सब करें, मन को बिरला कोई।
सब सिद्धि सहजे पाइए, जे मन जोगी होइ॥

माया मुई न मन मुआ, मरी मरी गया सरीर।
आसा त्रिसना न मुई, यों कही गए कबीर॥

Kabir Das explains that humans are so blind after physical needs and desires, decorate their body with ornaments, but never think of decorating their hearts and souls. He says that if we could decorate our minds and hearts with self-control, tolerance, self-analysis, loves and compassion—such beautiful ornaments—we can definitely achieve the ultimate goal of life and not only do our own welfare, but will also always think and could do something for the welfare of the others. Kabir Das stressed that while we live in this world, we cannot get away from all attachments, desires, and wants. This body dies number of times, but the wants, desires, and expectations of a human being never get satisfied and over for ever.

In recent years, there have been many studies that support the idea that developing compassion and altruism (unselfishness, humanity) has a positive impact on our physical and emotional health. Studies have shown that reaching out to help others can induce a feeling of happiness, a calmer mind, and less depression. We can discover the personal happiness in our own lives and the lives of those around us.

This is a paradoxical world. We human beings never follow our convictions and beliefs. When a person says, "I am an honest person", is he or she really honest in all situations? When a person talks of values, sympathy, compassion, we can see most of the time in his or her behaviour is totally opposite of what he or she believes about himself. Understanding the other person's problem, his or her critical state of mind, is this not a value? Speaking in a loving tone with everyone, so what if the person is poor or belongs to a low status, is this not a value? Being humble to everyone despite the high position we hold, is this not a value? It is very difficult to understand why people become so sadistic. They seek pleasure in hurting others; they feel happy in seeing others in pain. They are jealous of others' achievements. And we can see that such people are mostly talking of God, satsangs, and spirituality. There is a lot of confusion and conflicts in people's thoughts and actions. We don't follow our convictions and beliefs.

कथनी मीठी खांड सी, करनी विष की लोई।
कथनी छोड़ी करनी करे, विष का अमृत होई।।

Kabir says that we should always remain cautious of those people who speak in a sugar coated language, but their actions are very poisonous and harm others. They will create harmful conditions for other people while presenting a good image that people cannot even imagine in their dreams that this person can do such a negative thing.

जैसी करनी जासु की, तैसी भुगते सोय।
बिन सतगुरू की भक्ति के, जनम जनम दुख होय।।

Kabir says that what we sow, we reap. We need to be careful in what we think and what we do. We need to remember that the ultimate truth of every living being is death. So we should devote ourselves to the service of God. By following our Guru, the Divine Power, we should inculcate the true knowledge of karma.

जब तू आया जगत में, लोग हंसे तू रोय।
ऐसी करनी न करो, पीछे हंसे सब कोय।।

Kabir Das says that when a child is born, everyone is happy but the child cries. Now the ultimate goal of life to leave behind such actions which people will remember for ever even after our death. They should smile while remembering us.

There are people around us, who hold their heads high thinking that they always speak good words. But Kabir says these are illiterate people in the real sense, who do not understand the true meaning of devotion, dedication, compassion, and empathy. They just keep floating in a sense of pride. Kabir Das emphasizes that action is more important than words. There is also a saying, "Actions speak louder than words". Mostly people who speak big words, give lectures, talk of values, basically do not follow the same when it comes to actions or internalize these values. They are ignorant in the real sense. It has also been understood through ages that what we sow, so we reap. Whatever we do, we will definitely have to face its consequences some time. If our actions are good and wise, full of compassion, care, concern, and love for others, for sure we will get happiness and satisfaction, if not immediately then in the time to come.

कबीर करनी अपनी, कबहुं न निष्फल जाय।
सात समुद्र आड़ा पड़ै, मिलै अगाऊ आय।।

Kabir says that every action has its consequences, nothing can stop it. We experience this fact in our lives every day. Emotional intelligence emphasizes that we should always behave with others in the same manner as we would like them to behave with us. Psychology explains intelligence as an ability to think rationally, to act purposefully, and to deal effectively with the environment (Wechsler, 1944). Now, to act purposefully means to act in the right direction for the welfare of others, for larger society, and the community. It is only then that we can be called intelligent. On a similar plane, Emotional Intelligence is the ability to understand our and others' emotions, to always act in a manner that we give happiness to others. Also, an emotionally intelligent person acts according to his or her beliefs. There is a harmony and a balance about what he or she thinks and how he or she behaves. Basically, an emotionally intelligent person is a very good human being—*Ek acha insaan jo doosron ke dukha dard ko samajhta hai, sab ko sath main le kar chalta hai aur usme ahankaar lesh matra bhi nahi hota.*

बड़ा बड़ाई न करे, बड़ा न बोलै बोल।
हीरा मुख से ना कहै, लाख हमारा मोल।।

Kabir Das emphasizes that a good human being does not boast of his or her good qualities. Neither does he or she talk high of their ego or achievements. Just like a diamond does not express its value, which is in lakhs and crores, similarly the value of a good person is understood only by a wise person.

Good persons always keeps themselves open for improvement and growth. They accept criticisms positively, with an open heart and mind. They believes in growing forever, learning every moment of their lives. They understands that if people criticize them, it is for their own benefit. They seek to learn from others' experiences to improve their own personality.

निंदक नियरे राखिए, ऑंगन कुटी छवाय।
बिन पानी, साबुन बिना, निर्मल करे सुभाय।।

Kabir Das says that we should always remain close to people who criticize us, for such people clean our nature without the use of soap and water. An emotionally intelligent person takes criticisms positively. We should remember that when a person is criticized, it means that there is something in the person, some special quality, some potential for which he or she is criticized. We should learn to accept. To accept is one of the most important qualities of an emotionally intelligent person—accepting ourselves with all the positive and negative qualities and then accepting others as they are, because each one of us is unique.

The second important quality is to appreciate, to praise. Human beings have to make great efforts to appreciate others. There are some who are so negative that they cannot even appreciate themselves and their own qualities, what to talk of appreciating others for their achievements. Kabir says:

निंदक दूर न कीजिए, कीजै आदर मान।
निर्मल तन मन करै, बकै आन की आन।।

Kabir says that we should always appreciate people. Even if we are criticized, we should not feel low because by his or her criticisms, we can improve upon qualities to a great extent.

Kabir also says that we should keep checking our company. The persons we stay with, talk with, and interact with are very important and influence our personality to a large extent.

कबीर संगति साधु की, जो करी जाने कोय।
सकल बिरछ चंदन भये, बांस न चंदन होय।।

Kabir says that a person who keeps a good company, who stays with people who have a pure and divine soul, understands their qualities and their importance. The fragrance of the chandan (sandalwood) tree is so intense that even trees which are near it also start spreading the same perfume. But a tree of bamboo (baans) does not get influenced by the perfume of chandan. Kabir says that people who are egoistic and carry false ego do not change for better even in the company of good souls. Thus, Kabir says:

संगत कीजै साधु की, कभी न निष्फल होय।
लोहा पारस परस ते, सो भी कंचन होय।।

This means that we should always interact with divine and pure souls, with good people because that will never go waste. Just like by a simple touch of *paras mani* even iron turns into gold, similarly in the company of good people, even a bad person can turn into a pure soul.

It is a basic human nature that our happiness and sadness depend on external factors, especially on people around us. When people respect and praise us, we feel happy. But when we are criticized or condemned, we instantly feel sad and are filled with self-criticism. Kabir says that we, human beings, are too involved in *maya*. Human beings have been sent by God with a purpose and a goal. This goal is to serve others, give them love, care, and compassion. It is our duty to get out of this attachment and expectations and live a life of service and commitment.

> बड़ा हुआ तो क्या हुआ, जैसे पेड़ खजूर।
> पंथी को छाया नही, फल लागे अति दूर।।

Kabir Das says that such goodness is of no use if it is not for others' welfare, just like the khajoor (dates) tree, which is too tall to give shade and its fruits are also too high above the ground. It neither gives shade to the passers-by nor can a person eat its fruit. So it is of no good, no use. Similarly, a person who is just good at speaking fancy language and talks big but is shrewd by heart, is not good for others.

> माया तजि तो क्या भया, मान तजा नही जाये।
> मान बड़े मुनिवर गले, मान सबन को खाये।।

Kabir Das explains that if a person sacrifices all his or her assets, wealth, wife, or sons, it is not a big thing. The important thing is to sacrifice and get rid of our ego, the *ahankaar* which is there in this heart. This *ahankaar* is the most dangerous thing on this earth; it has destroyed many wise saints and intellectuals. Thus, no matter how much we become educated, no matter how much we gain the knowledge of the world but if there is no love, compassion and empathy, all education is a waste. This IQ cannot give us the ultimate peace and tranquillity. It is only EQ, only emotional connectedness with ourselves and the world that will ultimately help us in reaching our goal of life that is happiness.

The ultimate success and happiness in life depends upon cultivating Emotional Intelligence, which contributes 80% to our achievement in life. The rest 20% depends on out intellectual and technical competence. In today's knowledge and digitalized society, everyone knows everything about everything. There is nothing in this world that cannot be assessed, thanks to Google baba and technological advancements. But the predicament is, and as I have mentioned earlier, that humans are being driven away from themselves and others. Humans have, no doubt, become the masters of technology, but have also become servants of their emotions, weaknesses, and attitude. Tolerance, patience, compassion, connectedness, emotions, respect, care, love, and empathy—where are these values? *Are we really intelligent?*

I would like to share a case here. Once, a mother and father came to me for the counselling of their son who was studying in the seventh standard. The father was working at a very high and reputed post in a Government department. It was a very well to do family and the father was very well educated. The mother was a simple lady and was a housewife. This boy was the only child of his parents. The father and mother, in front of the child, started a list of complaints—he answers back, does not study, just wants to play, freaks out, and is always in bad company. The father said that he had provided him with all the amenities possible—chauffeur driven car, the most expensive mobile phone, i-pads, video games, and so on. He also said that he had tried everything with his son, but it was of no use. He had tried to explain him with love, he had beaten him, punished him to extreme extent, but the child was being more and more rebellious and his demands for the costliest technological gadgets was increasing day by day. "Ultimately, you are our last resort," he said. In this whole 20 minutes complaint *gatha*, I was observing the child sitting beside his father. The child was not feeling ashamed at all of anything. Instead, I could feel and understand a sense of achievement on his face and in his gestures.

Is this Emotional Intelligence on the part of mature parents to speak out the whole list of complaints in front of their child, who is still immature so innocent? The father's main emphasis was that "*Humne apne bache ko koi kami nahi rakhi, koi abhav nahi hai, jo mangta hai wo dete hain. To phir wo kehna kyon nahi manta hai? Jawab kyon deta hai, padhta kyon nahi hai?*"

No doubt, the parents did their best to fulfil all the materialistic and physical needs of the child, but what were they doing to meet the emotional needs of the child—his need for love, his need and right for quality time of his parents? Was this Emotional Intelligence? It was a total failure in their role as parents.

If the parents cannot connect with the child emotionally, are not aware of their needs and rights, have no quality time for their children, then these parents are not emotionally intelligent parents. What is the use of such education, such high qualifications, degrees, jobs, posts, amenities, if the child is not emotionally happy and not at peace?

I think this is the story of most of the families today. As I said in the beginning of the book, we are madly and badly running after money, name and fame, competition, and taking our relationships for granted. "*Hum budhimaan to bahut ho rahen hain par shayad humme samajhdari kaam ho rahi hai.*"

If any of such parents are reading this book, I request them to come out of the role of husband and wife and become parents. Parenting is a very responsible job. No child has ever asked his or her parents to bring him or her into this world. It is we, parents, who for the sake of our own interest and pleasure, bring this new life to this hard world. Every life, every existence, has its needs—both physical as well as emotional. No doubt, every parent tries his or her best to provide all that a child needs for his or her daily living, gets him or her admitted to the best of schools for best of education, makes arrangements for best of coaching and tuitions, and makes him or her join all kinds of extracurricular activities. But still, many times the child remains morose, depressed, *"gumsum"*, anxious, fearful, and insecure. Why?

There are frequent conflicts and fights between parents and adolescents. There are cases of families where the father, out of anger over his teenage son for some reason, punished him in such a way that the boy lost his one eye. My question is: Is this Emotional Intelligence where the father could not control his emotions and his anger? Without understanding, without connecting with the child, he started punishing him, and for what? Does this punishment lead to good behaviour of the child? Even if it is so, it is only temporary and not permanent, because this discipline is based on fear and disrespect. Actually, if we see within ourselves, we will find ourselves to be very selfish. We only want our own happiness, our satisfaction, we want to control others, we expect them to do what we want them to do, and not what they like.

प्रीति रीति सब अर्थ की, परमारथ की नाहिं।
कहैं कबीर परमारथी, बिरला कोई कलि माहिं।।

Kabir Das says that all love in this materialistic world is associated with selfishness. Every relation on this earth is standing on the foundation of selfish interests and expectations. It is related to wealth and selfish motives. We love others because, directly or indirectly, we are drawing favours from that person. There are very few exceptional people on this earth who are free from all selfishness and love others, free from all bondages, attachments and expectations. The world has become very selfish and materialistic.

We are becoming empty from inside because we are not pure in our feelings, in our desires; there is no satisfaction, just a burning desire for more and more. People are moving more towards materialism rather than spiritualism. Rich are becoming richer and poor are becoming poorer. Some important characteristics of an emotionally intelligent person are the qualities of openness, giving, sharing, and accepting. Instead of accumulating more and more for ourselves, we should learn to give more and more to others, be it love, happiness, a smile or wealth. Kabir says:

जो जल बाढ़े नाव में, घर में बाढ़ै दाम।
दोनों हाथ उलीचिये, यही सयानो काम।।

Kabir Das says that when water starts filling up a boat in a river, we start taking out that water as it is dangerous; similarly, if we start accumulating too much money in our home, we should not delay giving it away, before it is wasted. We should start giving that money with both hands. This is wisdom, otherwise we will develop vices like ego and greed. We should use our money to do good to others and use it for the welfare of the needy.

Kabir's philosophy is based on the concept of attaining enlightenment during our lifetime. Kabir views enlightenment as unifying with the four stages, that is, self-conceptualization, self-analysis, self-exploration, and self-realization. These are crucial for an individual in realizing the supreme power of mind, which is enlightenment. In order to attain enlightenment, it is essential for an individual to purify his or her soul, which means enhancing the positivity and reducing the negativity. This is the only way of developing a sense of morality and human values.

जो तू परा है फंद में, निकसेगा कब अंध।
माया मद तोकूं चढ़ा, मत भूले मतिमंद।।

Kabir Das stressed that we are tied up in the chains of worldly pleasures. We have forgotten everything because we have been blinded by the brightness of these worldly things—so much so that we have got disconnected even with ourselves. Kabir alerts us and says that we need to connect with ourselves so that we can achieve and connect with the ultimate Divine Power.

Anger Management

Another important parameter of attaining well being is to control our negative emotions like anger. Kabir says:

माटी कहे कुम्हार से, तू क्या रौंदे मोय।
एक दिन ऐसा आएगा, मैं रौंदूगी तोय।।

The mud and sand says to the potter that you are crushing me (mud) under your feet. Don't feel egoistic about it. Time does not remain the same for everyone. There will be a day when you will become part of me. Therefore, everyone should be humble and compassionate towards every other person.

Kabir again emphasizes:

जग में बैरी कोय नही, जो मन भीतल होय।
या आपा को डारि दे, दया करे सब कोय।।

He says that if our heart and mind is peaceful, we have no enemies because when we are angry or not at peace, we fall into unreasonable arguments with others and we fight. If we can control our emotions, anger, and hatred and be humble, everyone will show love, respect, and compassion towards us, and vice versa. Dale Carnegie also stressed, "The best way to get out of an argument is to avoid it."

वाद विवादे विश घना, बोले बहुत उपाध।
मौनि गहै सबकी सहै, सुमिरै नाम अगाध।।

Kabir emphasized that arguments are like poison. They hurt the ego and feelings of many people. Because of these hurt feelings, people become enemies of one another and there is negativity all around. The person who tolerates, remains quiet, and remembers the name of God, remains away from unreasonable arguments. He or she is a proactive person and, of course, an emotionally intelligent person.

Kabir Das says that anger is one emotion, but there are all kinds of negativities connected with anger—jealousy, greed, attachments, hatred, etc. When a person is in anger, all his or her good deeds get washed away and the person is seen as a bad person who has no control on his or her emotions. An emotionally intelligent person has control on his or her emotions. He or she knows when to be angry with the right person, at the right time, for the right reason, and for the right amount. We are very reactive people, always at the verge of acting out our emotions upon a small instigation. These reactions always put us in trouble. The concept of Emotional Intelligence emphasizes that a mentally healthy person is a proactive person rather than a reactive person. This means that in any situation, an Emotionally Intelligent person stops, thinks, analyses the situation and his or her thoughts, and then handles or deals with the situation as required. On the other hand, people who have no control on their emotions are very vulnerable, touchy, and intolerant. They react at once, get into trouble, and make their life and relationships miserable.

    We need to check our thoughts and our words at least every hour of our day, because what we think, so we feel and it ultimately reflects in our actions. Our mind and body work together. It is so simple. If we eat nutritious food, do regular physical exercises, yoga, pranayama, aerobics, go for walk—all this will surely keep our physical body healthy and fit. Similarly, it needs to be understood that having good thoughts, pure and divine feelings, reading good material, using positive words and messages with ourselves and others, will keep our mind in place and at peace, our attitude positive, and we will surely become a positive person, always sending positive vibrations to the people around us and to the world at large.

> जैसा भोजन खाइये, तैसा ही मन होय।
> जैसा पानी पीजिये, तैसी वाणी होय॥

    Kabir Das says that our thoughts depend on the food that we eat. Similarly, our *maan*, our language, and our tone depends on the kind of water we drink. (Maybe here Kabir Das is talking about those who eat too much non-vegetarian food). People who eat too much *tamasic* food are mostly negative and reactive and have a lot of anger in them. Also, people who are regular drinkers (alcoholic drinks) have no control on their words and make an exhibition of themselves. So, for our well being and well being of others, it is important we turn to *sattvic* vegetarian food.

    Traditionally, food is categorized into Tamasic, Rajasic, Sattvic, or a combination of them.

Tamasic

Tamasic foods are those that have a sedative effect on the mind and body. In general, they are considered detrimental to health. According to yoga, these foods are to be avoided as they can cause mental dullness and physical numbness. However, in times of pain they are allowed to alleviate suffering.

Examples of such food include meat of an animal, fish, fertilized egg, onion, garlic, scallion, leek, chive, mushroom, alcoholic beverages, durian, blue cheese, eggplant, opium, and any food which has been kept overnight before consumption.

Rajasic

Rajasic foods are those that have a stimulating effect on the mind and body. They are considered to be neither beneficial nor harmful. These foods lead to aggressiveness and irritability, and are often obtained in a way that harms another organism.

Examples of such food include caffeinated drinks (such as coffee, tea—both black and green, cola drinks, and energy drinks), brown or black chocolate, paan, ginkgo biloba, overly spicy food, salty food, and unfertilized egg.

Sattvic

Sattvic foods are those that lead to clarity of mind and physical health. These foods are to be consumed on a regular basis. Sattvic foods are generally those which can be obtained without harming either another organism or one's self. Only Sattvic foods are acceptable as offerings to the Hindu gods, with rare exceptions.

Examples of such food include water, cereal grains, legumes, vegetables, fruits, nuts, unpasteurized and unhomogenized fresh milk and all fresh milk derivatives like ghee, butter, cream, fresh or cottage cheese (paneer), and yogurt (lassi)), and raw honey.[21]

Kabir was strictly against the practice of hypocrisy and didn't like people maintaining double standards. He always preached people to be compassionate towards other living beings and practice true love. He urged the need to have the company of good people who adhere to values and principles.

Today, religion is misinterpreted and has become a means of violence and terrorism. This is a time when Kabir's philosophy is an enlightening source to describe humane behaviour by knowing the true meaning of religion. Religion is not about following rituals and ceremonies, but about purifying the soul by eradicating all the evils within. The essence of Kabir's philosophy lies in embracing the self and the humanity as a whole, which is possible only by developing Emotional Intelligence.

As mentioned earlier, Emotional Intelligence is an oxymoron. It is difficult for people to accept the fact that people can be intelligent emotionally as well as intellectually. However, after going through the nine realizations described in this book, I hope my friends have understood and realized that we can become intelligent emotionally, and how it is so important to be emotionally intelligent to be successful in life, in our career, and in our relationships. I have tried my best to make the concept simple through the dohas of Sant Kabir Das, who, in such a simple way, has emphasized the core of Emotional Intelligence.

There may be a number of loopholes in the content. I understand and accept them. I will appreciate if I can get your feedback so that I can improve and share my experiences and knowledge with the blessings of everyone.

---

21. http://hinduism.stackexchange.com/questions/2659/what-are-tamasic-rajasic-and-sattvic-foods(accessed on 06 March 2017).

Be Positive! Be Happy!

REALIZATIONS

1. Emotionally healthy people are in control of their emotions and their behaviours and are able to handle life's challenges, build strong relationships, and recover from setbacks.
2. The capacity to recognize our emotions and express them appropriately helps us to avoid getting stuck in depression, anxiety, and other negative mood states.
3. Having trusted people around with whom we can share our feelings, can also reduce stress to a great extent.
4. The best indicator of Emotional Intelligence is a positive attitude towards life. An emotionally intelligent person understands that this life is unique, given by the Almighty, and makes his or her best efforts to make the most of it.
5. We need to become more health conscious rather than disease conscious.

References

American Institutes for Research (AIR) (2005). Effects of Outdoor Education Programs for Children in California. Palo Alto, CA.

Cervinka, R., K. Röderer, and E. Hefler. (2012). Are nature lovers happy? On various indicators of well-being and connectedness with nature. *Journal of Health Psychology*, 17(3), 379–388.

Coley, R., F. E. Kuo, and W. C. Sullivan. (1997). Where does community grow? The social context created by nature in urban public housing. *Environment and Behavior*, 29(4), 468.

Hartig, T. (1991). Restorative effects of natural environment experiences. *Environment and Behavior*, 23, 3.

Louv, R. (2008). *Last Child in the Woods: Saving Our Children from Nature-Deficit Disorder*, Algonquin Books.

Mind Organization. (2007). *Ecotherapy: The green agenda for mental health*. UK: Mind Publications.

Mitchell, R., and F. Popham. (2008). Effect of exposure to natural environment on health inequalities: An observational population study. *Lancet*, 372(9650), 1655–1660.

Morrison, C., and H. Gore. (2010). Relationship between excessive internet use and depression: A questionnaire-based study of 1,319 young people and adults. *Psychopathology*, 43(2), 121–126.

Ulrich, R. S. (1984). View through a window may influence recovery from surgery. *Science*, 224(4647), 420–421.

Ulrich, R. S., R. F. Simons, B. D. Losito, E. Fiorito, M. A. Miles, and M. Zelson. (1991). Stress recovery during exposure to natural and urban environments. *Journal of Environmental Psychology*, 11(3), 201–230.

Weinstein, N. (2009). Can nature make us more caring? Effects of immersion in nature on intrinsic aspirations and generosity. *Personality and Social Psychology Bulletin*, 35, 1315.

Zelenski, J. M., and E. K. Nisbet. (2014). Happiness and Feeling Connected: The Distinct Role of Nature Relatedness. *Environment and Behavior*, 46(1), 3–23.

http://www.achhikhabar.com/2013/03/03/kabir-das-ke-dohe-with-meaning-in-hindi/ (accessed on 06 March 2017).

http://www.speakingtree.in/blog/kabir-das-ji-ke-dohe (accessed on 06 March 2017).

http://suvicharhindi.com/kabir-das-ke-dohe-hindi/ (accessed on 06 March 2017).

http://www.rapidleaks.com/india/these-11-couplets-of-kabir-das-will-change-how-you-look-at-life/ (accessed on 06 March 2017).

http://www.shishuworld.com/index.php/2011/09/22/kabir/ (accessed on 06 March 2017).